THE KEY TO HEAVEN

RAY COMFORT

Whitaker House

THE KEY TO HEAVEN

Ray Comfort
Living Waters Publications
P.O. Box 1172
Bellflower, CA 90706

ISBN: 0-88368-477-2
Printed in the United States of America

Whitaker House
30 Hunt Valley Circle
New Kensington, PA 15068

2 3 4 5 6 7 8 9 10 11 12 13 / 06 05 04 03 02 01 00 99 98 97

Contents

Foreword
1. You Really Had to Be There 9
2. Adam's Breath 21
3. The Next Logical Step 31
4. The Poison of Asps 46
5. Swift Destruction 53
6. Too Hot to Handle 67
7. The Wrong Door 79
8. Sleeping at the Wheel 87
9. Ahab's Wrinkled Brow 97
10. Let the Cock Crow 103
11. Fifteen Minutes to Die 111
12. From the Lips of Sinners 118
13. Ten Needle-sharp Claws 125
14. How the Masters Did It 139
15. Witnessing Using the Law 150
16. The *Jesus Satisfies* Gospel 172
Addendum 189

Foreword

The law of the LORD is perfect,
converting the soul.
—Psalm 19:7

I once came out of a store and saw a lady trying to open her car door by using a bent, wire coat-hanger. I asked if it was her car, or if she was stealing it. A smile relieved her face of obvious frustration. When I offered to help, she gladly handed me the coat-hanger.

It was apparent that the wire wasn't strong enough to grip the handle on the inside of the car door. So, as I chatted with the woman, I took some time in bending, twisting and shaping the wire so that it had both the strength, and the contours to grasp the handle. With great skill, I carefully lowered the newly-molded tool towards the handle, but to my embarrassment, the innovative instrument was now too short. It didn't even **reach** the handle!

It was then that I asked the woman to stand back. I was going to try my car keys in the car door. It was a long shot, but it would at least take attention off my obvious blunder. I slipped the key into the lock, then turned it, and to our total surprise and delight, the door immediately opened.

Modern evangelism has bent, twisted and shaped its methods in a sincere effort to unlock the heart of unbelievers. To the embarrassment of many, our efforts have fallen short of the ideal. Yet, the key to the sinner's heart is, and always has been, close at hand to the church. All it will take to open the door of revival is to abandon our own efforts and try the key to see if it does indeed work.

In a magazine called *American Horizons*, a mainline denomination in the United States published their church growth statistics for 1991. Out of a total of 11,500 assemblies, 7,872 responded to the questionnaire, and revealed that a massive 294,784 decisions were obtained during that year. Unfortunately, only 14,337 remained within the church. This massive loss of converts is typical of modern evangelism, where the average fallaway rate is around 80%. The author of the report said, "Something is wrong."

Something is wrong, and has been wrong for nearly one hundred years of evangelism, since the church forsook the key to the sinner's heart. It set aside the ten commandments in their function to convert the soul (Psalm 19:7) and to show us our true state, and thus see our need of God's forgiveness.

I have heard a number of preachers say that it is biblical normality to have 75% of those coming to Christ fall away. During the altar call, they know that only one in four of those responding to their message will go on in their faith. So they are more than likely not too alarmed by modern statistics which reveal an 80% failure rate. The basis for this thinking is that the parable of the sower shows only 25% of the crop were on good soil (Mark 4:1-20). But I am convinced that Jesus didn't give the parable as a consolation for disappointing evangelical results, but for our instruction.

When we study the parable closely, we see that the good soil hearer, the genuine convert, had some things the others didn't have. He had understanding (Matthew 13:23), and he had a good and honest heart (Luke 8:15). Does that mean that throughout humanity, there are those who somehow have understanding and a good and honest heart, and we have to keep on sowing until we find them? No, Scripture makes it clear that there is no one who understands (Romans 3:11), and that the heart of man is not honest, but deceitful and desperately wicked (Jeremiah 17:9).

How then did the genuine convert obtain these virtues? Something from without his own heart must have given him understanding and brought him to a point of having a good and honest heart. The *"schoolmaster"* (Galatians 3:24) taught him that his heart was wicked. The spade of the law turned the soil and exposed the stones of sin. When these were removed through repentance, it left the good soil of understanding and a heart that saw itself in truth. A person with a good and honest heart is merely someone who is honest about their own wickedness. Their mouth of justification has been stopped by the law (Romans 3:19). They can now receive the incorruptible seed of the Word of God, and it will bring forth fruit without hindrance. They are "*born-again, not of corruptible seed, but of incorruptible, by the word of God which lives and abides for ever*" (1 Peter 1:23). These are the ones who go their way and sin no more (1 John 3:9).

This was the key to the success of men like Charles Finney, who had a retaining rate of around 80% of those who came to the Savior under the message he preached. Finney thoroughly prepared the soil of the heart with the law, before planting the seed of the Gospel. That was the key of the masters of past centuries, and that same key to revival can be God's gift to us, if we will only pick it up and use it.

When we, as the church, return to the right application of the law, we will truly unleash the power of this great weapon against the kingdom of darkness. Many who are now in bondage will be set free when they come to a true comprehension of their need for a Savior. Then the correct use of the law will give Satan his biggest nightmare.

Dedication

This book is dedicated to my good friend,
Pastor Mike Smalley

Purpose

This publication has a two-fold purpose. It has been primarily written for those who have not yet made their *"calling and election sure"* (2 Peter 2:10), and also as a practical guide to the use of the law in evangelism.

Chapter One

You Really Had to Be There

When drunken cowboys shoot up the town, it's the law-abiding citizens who want the law to make its presence known. They want the town "cleaned up." More than ever before in history, the lawless are shooting up the town. We are seeing iniquity abound on every side. Riots, murder, rape and other familiar evils have suddenly brought the ten commandments in vogue. Ted Koppel, host of ABC's *Nightline,* said,

> We have actually convinced ourselves that slogans will save us. "Shoot up if you must, but use a clean needle." Or, "Enjoy sex whenever and withever you wish, but protect yourself." No! The answer is "No!" Not because it isn't cool or smart or because you might wind up in jail or dying in an AIDS ward, but because it's *wrong!*

> What Moses brought down from Mount Sinai were not ten suggestions, but ten commandments!

Actress Elizabeth Taylor, no doubt angered by the biblical stance on homosexuality, said of AIDS, "It's a disease. How dare these so-called religious people use the disease to discriminate against homosexuals! We're all God's children...**Whatever happened to compassion, and to caring, and to the ten commandments?"**

Most, like Liz Taylor, think that the reason God gave the ten commandments was to use as a "rule of thumb," a moral standard by which we are to live. When things get out of hand, they think the law will clean things up. That is understandable. If we want to live in peace and harmony, we should honor our parents, fear God, refrain from theft, lying, murder and greed, and the like. However, the Bible gives us insight as to the actual God-given purpose of those ten edicts, commonly referred to in Scripture, as the *"law of God."*

J.I. Packer, author of *Knowing God* and *Evangelism and the Sovereignty of God,* concludes, "Unless we see our shortcomings in the light of the law and holiness of God, we do not see them as sin at all." In the face of modern evangelical methods, he conveys, "To preach sin means not to make capital out of people's felt frailties (the brain-washer's trick), but to measure their lives by the holy law of God."

To summarize the biblical use of the law, let me quote from author and pastor David Wilkerson:

> Many "grace" preachers do away with the law before it can do its work of convicting of sin. We are not saved by the law—**but we are convinced of our sin by the law!** *"For by the law is the knowledge of sin"* (Romans 3:20). The law was sent *"that every mouth may be stopped, and all the world may become guilty before God"* (verse 19). *"The law was our schoolmaster to bring us unto Christ, that we might be justified by faith"* (Galatians 3:24). *"The law is holy...and just, and good. Was then that which is good made death unto me? God forbid. But sin, that it might appear sin, working death in me by that which is good; that sin by the commandment might become exceedingly sinful"* (Romans 7:12-13).
>
> Paul was saying, "I couldn't really confess my sins until I knew they were sins! I couldn't seek after the holiness of God until I saw how far from Him I was! The law hit home to me, destroying my nonchalance about sin. When I saw God's holiness by His commandments, **sin became utterly sinful to me!**" That is the conviction that drives you straight into the

arms of Christ, crying, "Mercy, Lord! I can't save myself, I can't fulfill Your law. I have seen the sin of my heart!"

Charles Spurgeon said, "The law demands perfection, but man has already fallen short of it; and therefore let him do his best, he cannot accomplish what is absolutely essential. The law is meant to lead the sinner to faith in Christ, by showing the impossibility of any other way. It is the black dog to fetch the sheep to the shepherd, the burning heat which drives the traveller to the shadow of the great rock in a weary land."

Many years ago, Dr. J. Gresham Machen wrote, "A new and more powerful proclamation of (the) law is perhaps the most pressing need of the hour; men would have little difficulty with the gospel if they had only learned the lesson of the law."

If God gave the ten commandments solely as a standard by which humanity is to live, why does history stand as testimony that they are not workable? All they do is stir in us *"all manner of evil desire"* (Romans 7:8). When Israel heard the law, they said they would obey it, but continually broke its perfect precepts, bringing God's wrath upon them. Why? Because they found what the Apostle Paul found—that all the law does is uncover sin in its true light.

The law is the surgeon's spotlight, which exposes the cancer that it might be removed by the sharp blade of the gospel. As the light of the law exposes the sinner's heart, he finds his mind agrees with the law. He has the "*work of the law written in his heart*" (Romans 2:15). His conscience bears witness that the law is good. He may even "*delight in the law of God after the inward man,*" but he finds another in his members, a law which Paul says, wars "*against the law of my mind, bringing me into captivity to the law of sin which is in my members.*" He finds the truth of the Savior's words, "*Whosoever serves sin is the slave of sin.*" He is held captive by the snare of the devil to do his will.

If God grants him repentance, his cry becomes, "*O wretched man that I am! Who will deliver me from this body of death?*" The law has done its work. It has made way for the Holy Spirit to convict of sin, righteousness and judgment. Now the skillful blade of the Surgeon may cut away the cancer.

This is what Watchman Nee is conveying in *A Table in the Wilderness* when he says:

> For we are all sinners by nature. The trouble is that without the law we do not know it. So long as God asks nothing of us, all seems to go well. It is when He demands of us something that the occasion

is provided for a grand display of our sinfulness, *"that through the commandment sin might become exceeding sinful."*

The Help of Moses

The law is our schoolmaster to bring us to Christ. The ministry of the law is like that of John the Baptist to Israel. His purpose was only to prepare sinners for the Messiah. The ten commandments are like ten road signs, all pointing to the Savior. They say with the Greeks who approached Philip, *"Sir, we would see Jesus"* (John 12:21). The law of God is like the central cross of Calvary that upheld the Lamb of God. It gives the reason "Christ must suffer." If there was no law, then there was no grounds for the cross.

It was there that *"righteousness and peace kissed each other"* (Psalm 85:10). The righteousness of the law of a holy God, and the peace of the gospel of grace embraced each other at Golgotha. Now God could freely give His favor to sinful humanity, the fruit of which would be the law written upon the hearts of men and women. Instead of being engraved upon stone and commanding obedience, it could now be written upon the heart of the new creation whose will is pliable to the law of God. These would obey, not because of the crack of the whip, but out of a broken spirit saturated in love. The cross breaks the heart, and the indwelling Spirit gives the desire to obey the Father's perfect will. After the Day of Pentecost, sinful Adam can now say with Jesus, *"I delight to do Your will, O my God... Your law is written in my heart"* (Psalm 40:8).

When Moses came down from the mountain with the God-given law in his hand, he found Israel wholly given to sin. He took the two tablets of stone and broke them into a thousand pieces at the feet of the children of Israel. What could they do? Could they pick up the shattered pieces and put the law together again? No. They needed someone who would make new tablets. Moses, by the sweat of his own brow cut two more tablets of stone.

Humanity has shattered the law into a thousand pieces; nothing we can do can put that law together again. It would take Another, who would sweat drops of blood, One who would offer His own body and soul to make things right with the law.

There may be another reason Moses had a part in cutting out the stone tablets upon which He rewrote the law. Why did He have Moses help? To show us that God condescends to use you and me to take the law in hand and preach it to the sinful masses. God and Moses prepared the law together, and the Spirit of God and the body of Christ can now use that same law as a schoolmaster to lead sinners to the Savior. He has committed unto us the word of reconciliation. When we preach sin, righteousness and judgment, we open the way for the Spirit to bring conviction to the heart of the sinner.

I Sure Wish I'd Been There

Allow your God-given imagination to run its course within the confines of Holy Scripture, and listen to someone who witnessed the giving of the ten commandments on Mount Sinai:

"My name is Jethro, but I'm sometimes known as 'Reuel.' I'm the father-in-law of Moses. We've become close, since he stood up to a gang of irritating shepherds, who drove my seven daughters away from watering my flocks. He even drew water for us—and the sheep. Moses seemed to like us, but then again, what man wouldn't like being surrounded by my seven beauties? But I did like him, and even gave him Zipporah to be his wife; they made me a grandfather.

"Moses didn't talk very much of his life in Egypt. He was a prince you know—quite a story. Apparently, he was a beautiful child and was saved from being murdered while he was still a baby. The Pharaoh was terrified that the

Hebrew slaves would rise up against him, so he decided to kill the potential men of war by murdering all the newborn male babies. Moses was placed in an ark made of bulrushes and put onto the river among the reeds. Pharaoh's daughter found him and adopted him.

"When, at 40 years old, he saw two of his Hebrew brethren fighting, he tried to stop them, and actually killed one of them. The King heard of this, so Moses fled from the face of Pharaoh. I can see why he wants to forget the past. He is not proud of his life in Egypt. He says he would rather *'suffer affliction with the people of God, than enjoy the pleasures of sin for a season'* (Hebrews 11:25). I know why too: he saw Him who is invisible—the God of Abraham. To live without regard to Him makes life futile. I have always said to my family, 'Why store up *"treasures on earth, where moth and rust destroy and where thieves break in and steal"* (Matthew 6:19)?' That's what I think the God of my fathers would say, if He were to speak to us.

"I will never forget the look on his face the day he told me of his first experience with God. (I was the priest of Midian at the time.) He'd been tending the flock on the back side of the desert at the base of Mount Horeb, when an Angel of the Lord appeared to him in a flame of fire out of the midst of a bush. He said the bush burned brightly with fire, yet it wasn't consumed—strange...said he was fascinated at first...and who wouldn't be! But when a Voice came out of the midst of the bush and called his name, he was terrified.

"It said, '*Do not draw near this place. Take your shoes off your feet, for the place where you stand is holy ground.*' It was the God of our fathers! He had seen the suffering of the children of Israel in Egypt and said He was going to deliver them, and take them into a land '*flowing with milk and honey.*'

"It was after that experience that Moses requested I let him return to those he left in Egypt. Forty years earlier he had thought that God would deliver them by his hand; it now looked like it was His timing. Forty long years of tending sheep had certainly changed him. He must've been the meekest man on earth. What could I say? God forbid that I should stand in the way of a man of faith.

"Then came those incredible plagues, the pillar of cloud, and then the deliverance through the Red Sea. How I wish I'd been there! Israel went through so much in those early days, and it began to show on the face of Moses; he looked so drawn out. I had to advise him to delegate, before he was worn out.

"What I missed seeing in Egypt was surely made up for by what I saw at the base of Mount Sinai. It was the third month from the departure from Israel. Moses spoke with God, and He told him how He bore us on eagles wings to bring us to Himself. He said that if we obeyed His voice, we would be a *'peculiar treasure to Him above all people...a kingdom of priests and a holy nation.'*

"He then told Moses that He was going to speak to all of Israel in three days. We were to prepare our hearts, wash our clothes and not even go near the base of the mountain—if we, or even an animal, touched the mountain, we were to be put to death! We weren't even allowed to go near our wives. I guess it was like a father, telling his children to put aside their pleasures because he wanted to reveal to them something exceptionally important.

"No words can express what I saw that day. You had to be there yourself. The thunder was so incredibly deafening, the flashes of lightning so dreadful, it put the fear of God in my heart. I thought to myself, *'Clouds and darkness surround Him; righteousness and justice are the foundation of His throne. A fire goes before Him and burns up all His enemies round about. His lightnings light the world; the earth sees and trembles. The mountains melt like wax at the presence of the LORD, at the presence of the LORD of the whole earth'* (Psalm 97:2-5).

"The mountain burned with fire, and yet at the same time there was a blackness and darkness like I had never seen. Then came the trumpet that was so loud, it could've raised the dead. It actually drowned out the thunder. I had never heard a sound of victory like it. It was the sound to herald in what came next. **The Voice.** The words seemed to rip through the very atoms of the universe. I was so scared, I glanced at Moses for some comfort. I looked into his widened eyes and heard him say, *'I am exceedingly fearful!'* I didn't feel at all comforted. Even though he was a *'friend of God,'* he, like me, was actually shaking with terror. Bear in mind, all this was happening when God wasn't even angry at humanity. He was just sharing His heart. What a terrible day the day of judgment will be, when the Almighty reveals His wrath.

"I will never forget that Voice. It made the thunder, the lightning, the blackness, and the sound of the trumpet, fade into obscurity. The earth shook with its din. The whole mountain trembled with each incredible word. All of us thought that we would die! **This was the Voice that spoke creation into existence!** This was the Supreme Creative Force that thundered through infinite nothingness and formed the suns, the planets, the mountains. This was the Holy One of Israel."

Chapter Two

Adam's Breath

You shall have no other gods before Me.
—Exodus 20:3

The year was 1491 B.C. The Almighty uttered His voice, and who was able to stand? He gave His mind to humanity. The Self-existent One spoke from heaven to the sinful sons of the adamic race. This was He whose finger painted the sunset, fashioned the baby within the womb; the One who formed its eyes, with their millions of microscopic light sensitive rods, created the blood, the hair, the flesh, the bones, the organs, the mind—with its incredible ability to reason. Yet that same mind, in its fallen state, can hardly begin to comprehend who, or what this God is.

What does this commandment mean, "*You shall have* ***no other gods*** *before Me*"? It means that in order of our affections, no one, and nothing should take the place of our Creator.

Probably the most obvious violator of this commandment would be the rich young ruler of Luke 18:18. Riches increased, and he set his heart upon them. (Psalm 62:10). His money made it "impossible" for him to enter the kingdom of God—a camel had more chance of slipping through the fine eye of a needle than this rich man had of entering God's kingdom. His self-righteous heart betrayed itself when he called Jesus *"good."* His loose use of the word received a rebuke from the Son of God, followed by the law in its capacity to act as a lamp. He was one who knew the commandments (verse 20), and said he kept at least the five that Jesus cited. Yet, one thing he lacked. He lacked obedience to the first commandment. His god was his money, and he could not serve God and mammon.

Adam paved the slippery and sinful path to hell, and the iniquitous feet of our forefathers have kept it smooth. *"By one man, sin entered the world, and death by sin"* (Romans 5:12). Although the law of Moses had not yet been given, Adam was held accountable for his sin. The Bible clearly says he was in *"transgression"* (Romans 5:14), which accordingly, means he was in "violation." What did he violate? He failed to choose God above himself. He had *"another god"* before Him. His actions showed that God was not his supreme authority. He chose the devil above the Lord. He listened to a lie rather than the truth. But more than that, the Scriptures tell us that Adam's sin was willful rebellion against God. He was not deceived as was his wife (1 Timothy 2:14). He walked into sin with his eyes wide open. He not only had an inner knowledge which was no doubt far superior to our fallen consciences, but he had a direct commandment from the mouth of God Himself. This command was Adam's ***"Thou shalt not"*** (Genesis 2:17), and he broke it into a thousand pieces.

Like all sin, his transgression had horrific repercussions. His trespass planted in us a sinful heart that would gladly break all ten of the commandments. We inherited Adam's sin. The kernel of sin deeply rooted itself in humanity and became a mighty tree of iniquity, reaching the high heavens.

If it were not for God's grace, the blind masses would prefer to be damned than obey God. I once stayed in a home where a Christian couple rarely watched their TV, but I turned it on after a meeting, to "wind down with the news." I flicked through the channels, and stopped for a moment on MTV, a channel I had never seen. A lead singer, well-dressed as far as rock stars go, was casually chatting with the crowd of about 50,000. He was using a slang term for a part of the female anatomy, saying how that's what he lived for and dreamed about. In a thirty-second period, he must have used the same swear word at least 6 or 7 times, as well as using other profanities. The crowd went wild with joy. With each expletive, hands and fists were raised in a show of unity for the love of sin. The irony was that the reaction was almost identical to Christians rejoicing in unified verbal praise to God.

Instead of feeling a sense of anger, I felt empathy for the man as he expressed his sinful adamic heart. His message, like a flame of lust, manifested the dark breast of the crowd. No longer did they hide the iniquity in the shadows, but as a "liberated generation," boldly made their passionate stand for sin.

Peter's penitent *"Depart from me, for I am a sinful man"* (Luke 5:8) can leave the ignorant with the impression that God is somehow like an innocent elderly woman, who, in her naivety is shocked by blatant wickedness. No, God knows what is in the heart of man. Rock singers who strut like proud roosters, spewing out their obscenities, may think they astound the heavens, but there is nothing new under the sun.

Sin is like bad breath. We can detect it in others, but rarely in ourselves. In fact God says our throat is like an open grave (Romans 3:13). I would love to have had a few minutes to speak to that crowd of 50,000. I would have reasoned with them, and shown them from Scripture that God knows their sin-filled hearts, that nothing is hidden from His eyes. Those that openly flaunt their iniquity are often easier to reach with reason than the self-righteous. To them it becomes obvious that the testimony of Scripture is true when it says we drink iniquity like water. They cannot deny they love darkness rather than light. What they don't see is the penalty for sin. They could not conceive for a moment that hell would be the just reward for their deeds.

This sex-craved generation of rebels has been left without law, something even the world is slowly beginning to see as illustrated in this statement in *The Wall Street Journal*:

> Sin isn't something many people spent much time worrying about in the past 25 years. But we will say this for sin: it at least offered a frame of reference for behavior. When the frame was dismantled during the sexual revolution, we lost the guidewire of personal responsibility, the rules for proper conduct in sexual relations. Everyone was left on his or on her own. It now appears many people could have used a road map. They needed to be told the direction their life was taking was simply wrong.

We have found ourselves on the wide path of Adam's avenue. The road map of the law shows us that we are heading for hell.

Adam blamed both God and Eve for his transgression when confronted by God. He said, *"The woman You gave to me..."* (Genesis 3:12). As far as he was concerned, it wasn't his fault. He was a willing victim of blind self-righteousness. The reason for this blindness is seen in the Word of God. The Bible reveals the problem: *"But sin, that it might appear sin..."* (Romans 7:13). If the law makes sin appear as sin, what does it masquerade as before it is exposed? The answer is comprehensive—weakness, failure, shoes too tight as a child, lack of self-esteem, inherited genes, dominant mother, aggressive father, no father figure, "the devil made me do it," "it's his fault," and "it's her fault." However, the law puts the blame where it lies, it thrusts the arrow of the finger of God at our wicked hearts.

The *"first Adam"* brought death upon humanity. The *"second Adam"* (Jesus Christ) brought us life. He kept the first commandment implicitly. What does it mean to walk in harmony with the law? Look to the life of the Son of God. Jesus delighted to do the Father's will, and the reason for this was that God's law was written upon His heart (Hebrews 10:7, Psalm 40:8). *"He was in all points tempted as we are, yet without sin"* (Hebrews 4:15). He loved his life as you and I love ours. Yet to do the Father's will, He was willing to give it in a most excruciating, bitter death.

Was His god His belly? No, even when the devil came to Him after a forty-day fast and tempted Him, He did not yield to the appetite for one moment.

Jesus of Nazareth loved God with all of His heart, all of His mind, all of His soul, and all of His strength, never seen more clearly than from the Garden of Gethsemane to the cross of Calvary. But He also loved His neighbor as Himself, seen by His teachings that gave a new meaning to the word *"love."* His concern for hungry multitudes, His touching of lepers, His gentleness with sinners, the raising of the dead, show a heart of compassion unsurpassed.

The cross of Calvary was the ultimate expression of both His love for the Father and His love for humanity. No greater love has a man than this. In studying His life, we have to agree with His own statement, *"I do always those things that please Him"* (John 8:29). His life, His death, and the resurrection of His body, give testimony that He was blameless before the first commandment.

How do we measure against the law? How do we measure up to the lifestyle of Jesus Christ? The *Westminster Confession of Faith*, which was written by godly men in 1646, made a statement in which they, using biblical basis for each directive, said what the first commandment entails. *The Larger Catechism* states:

> The duties required in the first commandment are, the knowing and acknowledging of God to be the only true God; and to worship and glorify Him accordingly, by thinking, meditating, remembering, highly esteeming, honoring, adoring, loving, desiring, fearing of Him, believing Him, trusting, hoping, delighting, rejoicing in Him, being zealous for Him, calling upon Him, giving all praise and thanks, and yielding all obedience and submission to Him with the whole man; being careful in all things to please Him, and sorrowful when in anything He is offended; and walking humbly with Him.

In the light of the spirituality of the law, we fall infinitely short of its just requirement. Do we measure up to the plumbline of the law's specifications? Do we love God with all of our heart, all of our mind, all of our soul and all of our strength? No, God's law is not written in our hearts; we don't delight to do His will. The law of sin and death has written its bloody signature on our godless breasts (Romans 7:21-24). Our natural cry is, "Not Your will, but mine, be done!" The devil is our father, and his will we do. The carnal mind is not subject to the law of God, neither indeed can it be.

I could see my own sinful heart tossed together with that great sea of humanity on MTV, in a tempest of rebellion, lifting high its foaming waves against God's law. But for the grace of God, there go you and I. I know what I am without His grace. I am willing to bet my boots that the crowd who so embraced the rock singer's words were not at all atheistic in belief. They no doubt believed in God, but were blinded by sin and self-righteousness into thinking that somehow He approved of their unlawful deeds. This generation has a form of godliness, but it lacks the true knowledge of God. Isaiah 29:13 is applicable when it says, *"Their fear toward Me is taught by the commandments of men."* How then is the fear of God taught? It is taught by the schoolmaster, God's law (Galatians 3:24).

Is our god our belly? We can find out by fasting, and see who holds the reigns of our appetites. Do we love the praise of men more than the praise of God? Do we love God with a passion? In truth, we struggle to even have faith in God. The test is what do we do with our time. Is it devoted to prayer? Who has our time: TV or God? What do we meditate on during the day or as we lay our heads upon our pillows at night? Is our delight in God who gave us life? Do we meditate on His Word both day and night? Could the Father say from heaven, *"This is my beloved son [or daughter] in whom I am well pleased"* (Matthew 3:17)? Do we love others as much as we love ourselves? Have we given ourselves in the service of others? Are we guilty of gossip, pride, self-esteem, envy, jealousy, hypocrisy? Are we *"perfect, as our Father in heaven is perfect"* (Matthew 5:48)?

The rich young ruler asked what good thing he had to do to get everlasting life. What "good thing" have we done today? Now, total up all our good works, let the Holy Spirit reveal our motives, and we will find we are no better than Adam, who tried to cover his shame with fig leaves. Scripture reveals that, without the grace of God, our attempts to do good are motivated by nothing but guilt, something referred to as *"an evil conscience"* (Hebrews 10:22), a guilt so evidently made clear by the first commandment, *"You shall have no other gods before Me."* We are weighed in the balance, and found infinitely wanting.

Chapter Three

The Next Logical Step

You shall not make for yourself any carved image, or any likeness of anything that is in heaven above, or that is in the earth beneath, or that is in the water under the earth; you shall not bow down to them or serve them. For I, the L*ORD your God, am a jealous God, visiting the iniquity of the fathers on the children to the third and fourth generations of those that hate Me, but showing mercy to thousands, to those who love Me and keep My commandments.*

—Exodus 20:4

As one reads the biblical account of perhaps the most infamous of all acts of idolatry —the making of the golden calf—it almost seems laughable. God delivered Israel by signs and wonders from Egypt. He then thundered His decrees from the holy mountain, the foundation of which forbad making and having other gods before the Lord. After hearing all the law from the mouth of Moses, the Scriptures tell us, *"And all the people answered with one voice, and said, 'All the words which the LORD has said, we will do'"* (Exodus 24:3). Yet, when Moses returned from the mountain with the two tablets of the law in his hand, he found the people worshiping another god—a graven image of the golden calf. How could this transpire? Aaron explained the mystery—when the children of Israel gave him their gold, he cast it into the fire, *"and there came out this calf"* (Exodus 32:24).

Idolatry comes naturally to the sons of Adam. Wherever the fires of lust burn, a golden idol emerges. As much as we would like to, sinful humanity cannot genuinely cling to the moronic belief that there is no God; so next on the list of philosophies that permit sin is idolatry.

Before we look at this topic in depth, let's look briefly at the number one preference for the license to sin—the subject of the denial of God's existence, atheism.

The issue is hardly dealt with at all in Scripture other than to say, *"The fool has said in his heart, 'There is no God'"* (Psalm 14:1). It is so absurd that it merits little response. If something is made, logic demands a maker. If something has "design," there must be a designer; and if there is a creation, there must be a Creator. The painting is absolute proof there is a painter. Yet, for some reason, most Christians feel intimidated by the professing atheist. They equate the belief with intellectualism. This assumption is erroneous.

This fact was clearly revealed in a recent article published by the American Atheist Society. In the article, the heart of atheism in America was made bare and seen to have a terminal disease. It was written by a particularly zealous (but somewhat discouraged) atheist, a graduate of the University of Texas and president of the American Atheist Society. He related five basic coronary problems plaguing contemporary atheists in the United States.

The first dilemma he cites within the stricken body of unbelievers is a **lack of unity**. He begins with a word on how unified Christians seem in their stand against abortion, and in the fact that they don't openly criticize one another. Then he says history has shown atheistic attitudes towards each other have been nothing but one of:

> Outright hostility...the Atheists [the author used caps] hate the agnostics, who hate the humanists, who cannot stand the rationalists, who keep their distance from the realists, who will not speak to the Unitarians, and on and on it goes...they

cannot even agree on the simple concept that 'there is no god.'"

The second symptom of the diseased heart of atheism in America, mentioned in the article, is one of a **lack of zeal**. The president says:

> Atheists will simply not get involved with the promotion of their chosen lifestyle. I cannot think of a group harder to motivate *[I can]*... Atheists seem to feel that their position with regard to religion is a deeply personal thing that does not need to be shared with others.

I suppose it is hard to be enthusiastic about the non-existence of God, when the word "enthusiasm" actually comes from two Greek words *en* and *theos* meaning "in God." If I denied the existence of the sun, I would find it rather difficult to be zealous in my convictions in the light of its brilliance.

The third dilemma is a **lack of faith**. He (no doubt with some shame) admits, "I have met many Atheists who cannot surpass the 'What if I am wrong?' stage."

Yes, atheists often doubt their doubts. Admittedly, there would be nothing more disconcerting than beginning to believe something you didn't believe was actually true. God knows, the root of their problem is merely a lack of unbelief.

The fourth ailment of the society is one of **lack of boldness.** He remarks about an incident where a newspaper reporter wanted to do an article on the subject of atheistic lifestyles: the atheist's president found nothing but the 'fear of man' in those whom he contacted. He said he called, "From person to person," and encountered, "such deep-seated fear that I could hardly believe my ears...in short, most of the Atheists I contacted were petrified with fear at being 'found out'...it was a climate of total fear."

And finally, he found that the average atheist was bound by a **lack of giving.** He speaks of generous Christians, and then protests, "I know that certainly there are persons of great means who are Atheists, but they simply will not assist in the struggle against religion...and I know you are out there..." He believes that they are out there, somewhere. Theirs is one existence that is not convenient to deny.

It seems that atheism in America has in past years, survived on a wing and a prayer. Now it has lost heart—the beat has stopped. Sadly for their leader, unless some sort of revival takes place, his frantic efforts at CPR are futile. Atheism in America is dead and should be quietly laid to rest.

Frankly, I love it when I meet someone who thinks he believes he is an atheist. He is like a foolish man who built his house on fresh air. Logic is his number one enemy. Those who deal in it, call his bluff. As I have said, logic demands that everything "made," must have a maker, and *therefore everything created must have a Creator*. To admit the first premise, but to deny the second is to move into an intellectual free zone.

Israel was not foolish enough to say that God didn't exist, especially in the light of the experiences they had been through. So, the next logical step for the sin-loving sons of Adam, was not atheism, but idolatry. The flame of lust instinctively produced a golden calf—they made a god to suit their sins.

It makes sense to the senseless to create a god in our own image—a god upon which we can direct our need to idolize, but a god who won't dictate any moral ethic—a god we can shape to our iniquities.

Unregenerate man has an affinity with his father, the devil. He loves to sin and is devoutly devoted to darkness rather than light. He is like behemoth, who drinks up a river of sin in a gulp: he guzzles iniquity like water. But like Israel and her golden image, his idolatry will leave him naked before God.

I was once an idolater. I didn't shape a god with my hands, but I definitely shaped one with my mind. I prayed to a god of my own creation. My unstated philosophy was, "My God would never create hell. My God is a God of love and mercy." No statement could be more truthful. My god would never create hell because he could not—he didn't exist. He was a figment of my imagination, the place of imagery. With such a belief, I could look at creation, give a measure of thanks to my 'creator,' and carry on in my sins.

This commandment reveals to us the incredible depth of the love of God for you and me. He is jealous for our love, and the thing that provokes His jealousy is idolatry. This sin is so serious in His sight that He will visit *"the iniquity of the fathers on the children to the third and fourth generations"* of those that hate Him. The root of idolatry is fueled by hostility towards God.

The Scriptures tell us that not only is humanity's hatred of God unjustified (they hate God "without cause"), but they reveal the point of contention between God and man:

> *Because the carnal mind is enmity against God; for it is not subject to the law of God, nor indeed can be.* (Romans 8:7)

Why do criminals hate the police? Because they are the upholders of civil law. If there were no civil law, no point of contention between law-breakers and law-enforcers would exist. If there were no law, there would be no enmity between man and God. Thus a law-less god is so attractive to unregenerate man.

What does it mean that God *"visits the iniquity of the father's on the children of the third and fourth generation?"* Jeremiah reiterates this Scripture when he says:

> *Ah, LORD God! Behold, You have made the heavens and the earth by Your great power and outstretched arm. There is nothing too hard for You. You show lovingkindness to thousands, and repay the iniquity of the fathers into the bosom of their children after them—the Great and Mighty God, whose name is the LORD of Hosts.*
>
> *(Jeremiah 32:17-18)*

In Lamentations 5:7 it says, *"Our fathers sinned and are no more, but we bear their iniquities."* Does it mean that the children suffer for the sins of the fathers? No, the Bible makes it very clear that God doesn't punish the children for the sins of their fathers (Ezekiel 18:19-20, Deuteronomy 24:16). The answer comes from a right understanding of the word "iniquity." It is *anomia* in Greek, and means "without law." When a father lives without regard to the law of God, it has a natural repercussion upon his offspring. By merely following his natural godless instincts, ways that may "seem right" to him, he not only leads his children to damnation in the next life, but he carves out a path for them this side of death. If he lives a godless life, unless God's grace intervenes, his children will also be godless and bring upon themselves and their own children the fruit of sin. The world cites "genes" as the cause of inherited tendencies towards alcoholism, suicide, obesity, divorce, anger, etc. The Bible cites the iniquity of the fathers.

In this commandment and in other portions of Scripture, we see both the *"goodness and severity of God"* (Romans 11:22). We are either under wrath or mercy: *"but showing mercy to thousands, to those who love Me and keep My commandments"* (Exodus 20:6).

> *[God] will render to each one according to his deeds: eternal life to those who by patient continuance in doing good seek for glory, honor, and immortality; but to those who are self-seeking and do not obey the truth, but obey unrighteousness—indignation and wrath, tribulation and anguish, on every soul of man who does evil, of the Jew first and also of the Greek.*
>
> *(Romans 2:6-9)*

Sin, especially sexual sin, is almost always the willing bedfellow of idolatry. One obvious example is seen in the issue of homosexuality.

In Romans, chapter 1, Paul speaks of God's wrath being revealed from heaven against all unrighteousness, because we sin willfully against the inner knowledge He has given us. But more than that: God has shown us of His existence through creation, so each of us are *"without excuse"* (verse 20). The natural progression from a denial of this inner knowledge will be idolatry (verse 23-25), and from there will come an unashamed manifestation of the *"vile passions"* of homosexuality and general lawlessness (verse 29-32). The way to awaken a homosexual to his sin is to show him the ten commandments (1 Timothy 1:10).

Idolatry can be very subtle. Paul spoke in Scripture of *"another Jesus,"* a non-existent savior created by sinful minds. A classic example of this can be seen in a tract published by a homosexual church in Los Angeles. The publication, which is called, "Homosexuality, Not a Sin, Not a Sickness," attempts to use a number of Scriptures to justify their immoral lifestyle, then concludes with:

> Thousands of lesbians and gay men, along with many friends and family members, have discovered new freedom and deep inner peace in a personal relationship with Jesus Christ...it is important for you to know that Jesus Christ died to take away your sins, not your sexuality. Christ accepts you as you are, and so do we.

Idolatry and deception go hand in hand:

> *Take heed to yourselves,* ***lest your heart be deceived, and you turn aside and serve other gods and worship them,*** *lest the LORD's anger be aroused against you, and He shut up the heavens so that there be no rain, and the land yield no produce, and you perish quickly from the good land which the LORD is giving you. (Deuteronomy 11:16-17, emphasis added)*

With all his godly wisdom, Solomon still fell into the arms of idolatry. Love of foreign women was the root of his sin, and archaeology has uncovered the fact that much of the idolatry of biblical times was accompanied by gross sexual perversions.

Paul used the law of God to alert the Athenians to their folly, when he saw that the whole city was given to idolatry. He first related to them, by quoting an inscription from one of their altars, then he preached the nature of the God of Genesis (Acts 17:24), His omnipotence (verses 25-26), His omnipresence (verse 28), and His omniscience (verse 30). Then Paul proclaimed the essence of the first and the second of the ten commandments. He virtually said, "There is one God; you shall have no other gods before Him, nor shall you make yourselves a graven image." He told them they needed to repent, because God had appointed a day in which He would judge the world in righteousness, by Jesus Christ.

I recently saw a video that probably would make the hair stand up on the necks of most evangelical Christians. It documented two missionaries' efforts to evangelize a primitive and no doubt, idolatrous tribe in the depths of New Guinea. They began by learning their culture, eating their food and building their trust. Then they launched their evangelical endeavors by teaching from the Old Testament. In fact, they **didn't mention Jesus for two months!** Instead, one of them related the story of Abraham and Isaac. When Abraham was about to sacrifice his son, the primitives said that God would intervene and provide a sacrifice. The missionary taught the law of Moses and the necessity for blood sacrifice so that sin could be forgiven.

After the foundation of the law and the prophets, he presented Jesus to them, who immediately became the village hero. Then, much to their horror, he presented the Sinless One being taken by wicked hands and crucified. To give them something visual, he had one of their number stand with his arms outstretched in a position of crucifixion; he then punctured a bag of red dye, which was concealed under the man's shirt. The natives immediately cried out, *"The Lamb!"* and became very sober as they heard that the Savior suffered for them. Suddenly, after a time of deep solemnity, they burst into spontaneous dancing for more than two hours as they realized the joy of their salvation. They even carried the missionary shoulder height in their rejoicing. That's biblical evangelism.

There is No Other

God's law exposes the error of idolatry to which we are all so prone. In fact, sin carries with it such a blind deception, even those of us who humbly pride ourselves in knowing the one and only true God are warned, *"Little children, keep yourself from idols"* (1 John 5:21). Beware, the minute you and I fall into sin, we are prone to idolatry.

The irony of idolatry is that there are no other gods, in the sense that there is only one Creator. *"Is there a God beside Me? Indeed there is no other Rock; I know not one"* (Isaiah 44:8):

> *For thus says the LORD, who created the heavens, who is God, who formed the earth and made it, who has established it, who did not create it in vain, who formed it to be inhabited: I am the LORD, and there is no other.* *(Isaiah 45:18)*

A scribe once came to Jesus and asked Him which is the first or the greatest commandment of all. Jesus said:

> *The first of all the commandments is, Hear, O Israel, the LORD our God, the LORD is One. And you shall love the LORD your God with all your heart, with all your soul, with all your mind, and with all your strength. This is the first commandment. And the second, like it, is this: You shall love your neighbor as yourself. There is no other commandment greater than these.*
>
> *(Mark 12:29-31)*

Jesus said these two were one commandment. They cannot be separated. We are commanded to love God, and we are also commanded to love our neighbor as much as we love ourselves. Who is my neighbor? He is the stranger on the road to Jericho—anyone who we meet who has a need. The stranger, who had been beaten and robbed as he made his way to Jericho, had his wounds gently attended to, and money was given freely to make sure he was taken care of. How far we fall short of this standard.

This Creator God, this Supreme Ruler of the Universe is holy and righteous. The first commandment is an edict we have all violated. We have an endless list of gods we have made in our own image, from the bearded old man reaching out to Adam, to man-made religions with millions of gods, to false images of Jesus, something Scripture calls *"another Jesus"* (2 Corinthians 11:4).

God warns that He will *"by no means clear the guilty"* (Exodus 34:7). In fact, He has a violent passion for justice. How fearful for sin-loving sinners to fall into His holy hands. Idolaters will not inherit the kingdom of God (1 Corinthians 6:9).

Chapter Four
The Poison of Asps

You shall not take the name of the LORD your God in vain, for the LORD will not hold him guiltless who takes His name in vain.
—Exodus 20:7

I was a Christian, yet I was sitting watching what was proving to be an X-rated movie! The year was 1978. I had received much publicity for my first book, and also because I had opened a drug prevention center to warn people of the dangers of drug abuse. One day, I received an invitation from a film company to view a new movie. They also invited the local drug squad. This was the deal: If I would publicly endorse the movie (which they thought had an anti-drug message), they would have a premiere and let me preach to the packed theater after the screening. I declined the invitation. The story-line was powerful, but the language (not to mention the violence) was something I could not encourage people to see.

The thing that remained fixed in my mind, was the fact that when someone in the film wanted to express disgust, right in the middle of profanities, he would use the name of Jesus. It really doesn't make any sense that people use the name of God to curse.

Often you will find that foul-mouthed, tattooed, hard-hearted bikers have a soft spot for their mother. On one arm they will tattoo the image of the devil, and the other arm will have a love-heart and the word "Mom." If you want to show your contempt for the biker, one effective way would be to speak ill of his mother.

In the same way, using God's name in profanity epitomizes the enmity between man and God. It is perhaps the most simple and effective way a man can show his contempt towards God. This is why it carries with it the death penalty under the law.

God's name is so holy, godly Jews won't even let it pass through their sinful lips. To say that His name is singularly distinct is a gross understatement. To even say that His name is holy doesn't convey what it should to our deafened ears.

When Moses had the unspeakable privilege of not only speaking with God, but of having the Lord actually give him his heart's desire (to look upon His glory), God said:

I will make My goodness pass before you, and I will proclaim the name of the LORD before you. (Exodus 33:19)

His name and His glory are synonymous. How can we give God's name honor? By listening to the law. He said to Israel:

If you do not carefully observe all the words of this law that are written in this book, that you may fear this glorious and awesome name, the LORD your God, then the LORD will bring upon you and your descendants extraordinary plagues... (Deuteronomy 28:58)

One reason we are seeing an increase in blasphemy (not only using God's name to curse, but evil speaking and mockery of God) is because of the blatant hypocrisy within the church. If the church doesn't exhibit a fear of God, why should the world revere His name?

King David's hypocrisy caused the enemies of the Lord to blaspheme (2 Samuel 12:14). Paul said to the Jews who broke the law, when they boasted that they kept the law:

For "The name of God is blasphemed among the Gentiles because of you," as it is written. (Romans 2:24)

How can unregenerate man fear a God they think condones sin? How can they fear a Supreme Being who is portrayed from many pulpits as having no sense of justice? He is merely a God who is there for the happiness of humanity.

If they don't hear the law, they will in their blind ignorance continue to sin and use God's name in contempt. Their transgression is not condonable, but it is understandable. The god preached from many a pulpit is not worthy of respect.

The law produces a fear of God that no other teaching can. The law helps us understand the attributes of God's character. It enables us see our own inadequacies, making us trust in grace. The fear of God and the hallowing of His name go hand in hand. No man can fear God and use His name in vain.

God's blessing of children should birth within us the fear of the Lord. What greater gift outside of the cross can God give to a man and a woman other than children? The Lord said to Jacob:

> *But when he sees his children, the work of My hands, in his midst, they will hallow My name, and hallow the Holy One of Jacob, and fear the God of Israel.*
>
> *(Isaiah 29:23)*

Blasphemers will not inherit heaven. The Lord will not hold him guiltless who takes His name in vain. Every idle word a man speaks, he will give an account thereof on the day of judgment, how much more those who have despised and cursed the name of the God who gave them life! In that day, the ten commandments of God's law will do their fearful work. It will be the same law that cast the stones at the man *"whose father was an Egyptian"* (Leviticus 24:10) in Israel:

> *And the LORD spoke to Moses, saying, "Take outside the camp him who has cursed: then let all who heard him lay hands on his head, and let all the congregation stone him. Then you shall speak to the children of Israel, saying: 'Whoever curses his God shall bear his sin, and whoever blasphemes the name of the LORD shall surely be put to death, and all the congregation shall certainly stone him, the stranger as well as him who is born in the land. When he blasphemes the name of the LORD, he shall be put to death.'"*
>
> *(Leviticus 24:13-16)*

The Bible warns, *"As many as have sinned in the law will be judged by the law"* (Romans 2:12).

When *"God was manifested in the flesh"* (1 Timothy 3:16) and became obedient to the death of the cross, *"God highly exalted Him and gave Him a name that is above every name: that at the name of Jesus every knee should bow..."* (Philippians 2:9-10).

The fact that men blaspheme the name of Jesus is testimony to the incarnation. They hate God without cause, and therefore hate Him who is the expressed image of the Father. God gave Him a name which is above every name. In fact, Scripture says His name is *"wonderful"* (Isaiah 9:6).

Jesus hallowed God's name like no other. When He prayed in John 17, He lifted His holy eyes to heaven and said, *"Father, the hour has come. Glorify Your Son, that Your Son may glorify You."* His very existence on earth was to bring the Father glory. He said, *"I have manifested Your name to the men You have given Me out of the world...Holy Father...while I was with them in the world, I kept them in Your name...O Righteous Father...I have declared to them Your name..."* (John 17:1, 6, 12, 26).

The Psalmist calls God's name *"excellent"*: *"O LORD our LORD, how excellent is Your name in all the earth,"* then he speaks of God's incredible goodness to man and concludes with, *"O LORD our LORD, how excellent is Your name in all the earth"* (Psalm 8:1, 9). Our praise for our God should be wrapped in the fear of His mighty and wonderful name.

When His disciples asked Jesus how they should pray, the first thing He taught them was to hallow the Father's name.

God's kingdom will only come to those who venerate His name. But do we do that? Do we give God's name the honor due to it? Do we love His holy name? Or do we let God's name roll off our lips without being worthy of a second thought? It means so little to us that "My God!" or "Jeeez!" and other obvious perversions of His name are vocalized in vain. Scripture paints a grim picture of us. It says, *"The poison of asps is under their lips, whose mouth is full of cursing and bitterness"* (Romans 3:13).

Isaiah said that he was a man of unclean lips, from a people of unclean lips (Isaiah 6:5). Our words merely speak the abundance of our ungodly hearts. Not one of us can look into the *"perfect law of liberty"* (James 1:25) and see the true image of our sinful hearts, without saying, *"God be merciful to me, a sinner"* (Luke 18:13).

Chapter Five
Swift Destruction

Remember the Sabbath day, to keep it holy. Six days you shall labor and do all your work, but the seventh day is the Sabbath of the LORD your God. In it you shall do no work: you, nor your son, nor your daughter, nor your manservant, nor your maidservant, nor your cattle, nor your stranger who is within your gates. For in six days the LORD made the heavens and the earth, the sea, and all that is in them, and rested on the seventh day. Therefore the LORD blessed the Sabbath day and hallowed it.
—Exodus 20:8-11

When God spoke to Moses about Israel's attitude to the Sabbath, He said these sobering words, "*You shall keep the Sabbath, therefore, for it is holy to you. Everyone who profanes it shall surely be put to death; for whoever does any work on it, that person shall be cut off from the people*" (Exodus 31:14).

The Sabbath was given as *"a sign between Me and the children of Israel forever"* (verse 17), something we still see which separates Israel from the whole Gentile world.

In the book of Numbers we read:

> *Now while the children of Israel were in the wilderness, they found a man gathering sticks on the Sabbath day. And those who found him gathering sticks brought him to Moses and Aaron, and to all the congregation. They put him under guard, because it had not been explained what should be done to him. Then the LORD said to Moses, "The man must surely be put to death; all the congregation shall stone him with stones outside the camp." So, as the LORD commanded Moses, all the congregation brought him outside the camp and stoned him with stones, and he died.*
>
> *(Numbers 15:32-36)*

When I read passages like this, I thank God I am not under law, but under grace. I am so thankful for the Savior's shed blood. My heart shudders for those who are still in their sins, for we see here a glimpse of the holiness of our Creator. Here is an instance of *"anyone who rejected Moses' law dies without mercy on the testimony of two or three witnesses"* (Hebrews 10:28). If mere disobedience to the law of the Sabbath, where a man preferred to work than rest, brought such swift and terrible punishment, how great will be the fate of the average sin-loving person, who transgresses the law many times daily.

This commandment is one you and I cannot keep because we have already transgressed its holy commission. We have already "gathered sticks" on the Sabbath, and we should therefore let the law, as a "*schoolmaster,*" drive us to Christ. In Him we will find the true rest:

> *For we who have believed do enter that rest, as He has said: "So I swore in My wrath, they shall not enter My rest," although the works were finished from the foundation of the world. For He has spoken in a certain place of the seventh day in this way: "And God rested on the seventh day from all His works"; and again in this place: "They shall not enter My rest." Since therefore it remains that some must enter it, and those to whom it was first preached did not enter because of disobedience, again He designates a certain day, saying in David, "Today," after such a long time, as it has been said: "Today if you hear His voice, Do not harden your hearts." For if Joshua had given them rest, then he would not afterward have spoken of another day. There remains therefore a rest for the people of God. For he who has entered His rest has himself ceased from his works as God did from His.* (*Hebrews 4:3-10*)

The moment we repent and put our faith in Jesus Christ, the Sabbath law is satisfied. No longer are we bound to labor to keep a certain day in order to be saved. If we have to keep a certain day to be justified, we have fallen from grace, and therefore are obligated to keep the whole law. We have become as the *"foolish"* and *"bewitched"* (Galatians 3:1). In fact, if we even listen to a person who says we should keep a certain day, we are disobeying Scripture. (See Colossians 2:16.) There isn't even one hint of a commandment in the New Testament for Christians to keep the Jewish Sabbath. If there was one, I would gladly rest on that day. If a Christian prefers to esteem one day above another, that's between him and God, and he has no right to press that conviction on another brother or sister (Romans 14:4-6; Acts 15:10-29).

According to the only authority we have, the disciples kept the first day of the week (Acts 20:7; 1 Corinthians 16:1-2), and we should follow their example.

The man who keeps the Sabbath, not seeking justification, but out of common sense, will find that there is *"great reward"* for doing so:

> *The law of the LORD is perfect, converting the soul; the testimony of the LORD is sure, making wise the simple; the statutes of the*

LORD are right, rejoicing the heart; the commandment of the LORD is pure, enlightening the eyes; the fear of the LORD is clean, enduring forever; the judgments of the LORD are true and righteous altogether. More to be desired are they than gold, yea much fine gold; sweeter than honey and the honeycomb. Moreover by them Your servant is warned, and in keeping them there is great reward.

(Psalm 19:7-11)

Farmers know that to bring out the best in soil, it should be rested for one year out of seven. God created man with the same need of rest. Never before have we had life so easy, with escalators, moving sidewalks, doors that open automatically, remote controls so that we merely have to move a finger to change the channel on television, microwaves to give us instant food, electric toothbrushes, calculators, word processors, instant photocopiers. Never before have we had so many time-savers, and never before has there been so much stress and burnout in society. The problem is that the farmer is exhausting the soil. He who rests one day in seven will reap the benefit of a fruitful life.

Charles Spurgeon, "the Prince of Preachers," is quoted in *Spurgeon at His Best* as having said the following:

> I am no preacher of the old legal Sabbath. I am a preacher of the gospel. The Sabbath of the Jew is to him a task; the Lord's Day of the Christian, the first day of the week, is to him a joy, a day of rest, of peace, and of thanksgiving. And if you Christian men can earnestly drive away all distractions, so that you can really rest today, it will be good for your bodies, good for your souls, good mentally, good spiritually, good temporally, and good eternally.

This is not the only commandment that offers great reward if kept. Looking at this purely from a practical standpoint, here are some other benefits of keeping God's law: Those who obey the commandments will do all things in the light of God's lordship. They love God and therefore will have regard to His reaction to every word, every deed and every thought. The godly person will say:

> *Let the words of my mouth and the meditations of my heart be acceptable in your sight, O LORD.* *(Psalm 19:14)*

From this will issue a lifestyle of holiness. He will keep himself from the world and therefore be free from polluting his body with cigarettes, and from the many adverse effects of illicit drugs. He will also keep away from the poison of alcohol. Few realize the misery caused by abuse of this drink:

> Alcohol, in excess, is by far the most devastating of drugs—wrecking families and friendships, impairing health, filling jails, hospitals and morgues. In 1990, it cost American society an estimated 130 billion dollars and more than 65,000 lives, 22,000 of them on highways. Heavy drinking can bring on brain damage, gastritis, pancreatitis, anxiety, malnutrition. It can depress the immune system. Alcohol can (also) exert nearly satanic power.
> (*National Geographic*, February 1992)

The godly will possess his body in honor and be free from sexual sin, avoiding AIDS and other sexually transmitted diseases. An estimated 25 million people will have AIDS by the year 2,000.

The godly man will not covet material things and save himself from discontentment. His god will not be mammon, therefore he will be free from greed and the vice of gambling. This will keep him from the burden of debt. He will keep his heart from the consuming passions of ambition that so often destroys relationships.

He will keep his word and develop faithful friendships. He will avoid the venoms of hatred and bitterness, which destroy men's bodies as well as their souls. He will love his wife as Christ loved the church, and thus reap the many benefits of a good marriage.

But there are even more advantages to be gained for living by godly principles. In California recently, two ironic situations occurred. The first was something that makes every parent shudder. A father, who was about to drive onto the freeway, for some reason put his baby (who was strapped into a portable crib) onto the roof of his car. He then leaned into the back seat to attend to another child. After this, he got into the car and drove onto the freeway. The only thing he neglected to do, was to put the baby in the car. It was still on the roof! Incredibly, the baby stayed on the roof of the vehicle as it went up the on-ramp, but fell off a little later onto the busy freeway. A motorist saw what he thought was a doll on the roadway, stopped, picked up the child and returned it to the father, unharmed. I'm sure the father thanked God from his heart.

Around the same time, a small child was sitting safely in a wooden-framed bus with his family. Suddenly a tire burst. The outer rubber shell broke through the floor of the vehicle, wrapped itself around the toddler, and pulled him onto the busy freeway. The child was tragically killed. What do you say to the mother? One can only hope that she had faith in God that would conquer her questioning as to why fate dealt her such an unfair blow. Her faith could lift her above her pains and say that the child was seen as a gift from God, whom God, in His great wisdom, allowed to be taken in such a terrible way.

Those who do have faith and walk in the law of the Lord will *"keep themselves from...idols"* (Acts 21:25). They won't let anything, including their love for their children, come above their love for God. In doing so, they will save themselves from much suffering. The person who puts God above all things, will bow the knee to His sovereignty. He will see that the *"king's heart is in the hand of the LORD... He turns it wherever He wishes"* (Proverbs 21:1). It will not be an offense to him that God governs the affairs of man. His faith in God lifts him above natural reasoning. Through faith in His exceeding great and precious promises, he knows that whatever happens to him comes by permission of his God, and therefore he rejoices that *"all things work together for good to those that love God, to those who are called according to His purposes"* (Romans 8:28). So, if life gives him a raw deal, he gives God the sacrifice of praise. Lion's dens, Red Seas and fiery furnaces are places of trial, of suffering, but never of despair. In the same circumstances, the world becomes confused, bitter, angry, and sorrows unto death; but the Christian overcomes in Christ. His heart is steadfast. In doing so, he saves himself from great anguish of heart.

More Great Rewards

One utter tragedy of sin is that when the ungodly live in willful darkness, they will have no reason for existence, something the end of which produces utter despair. A 12th Century poet put it this way:

> Drink! for you know not whence you came, nor why.
> Drink! for you know not why you go, nor where.

The life of the godly, however, will be free from futility, because of the victory he has over death through the cross. His eyes have been opened to the spiritual battle and to the existence of satan, who came to kill, steal and destroy. Therefore he is aware of the devil's desire to destroy him through the pleasures and temptations of sin and the world.

He has a joy unspeakable because his name is written in heaven. The cross is ever before his eyes—the love of his God has been made manifest. He knows from experience that *"godliness with contentment is great gain... having promise both in this life, and in the life to come"* (1 Timothy 6:6; 4:8)

Can you imagine what a blessed state a nation would be in if it kept the law of God? Imagine having no theft, no murder, no violence, no adultery, because no one would covet other people's things. They would love their neighbors as they loved themselves and treat them accordingly. There would be no drunk drivers, no alcoholics or drug addicts, no rapists, no prostitutes, no gangs, and therefore no need for America's 17,000 police agencies.

The Bible says:

> *He who loves another has fulfilled the law. For the commandments, "You shall not commit adultery," "You shall not murder," "You shall not steal," "You shall not bear false witness," "You shall not covet," and if there is any other commandment, are all summed up in this saying, namely, "You shall love your neighbor as yourself." Love does no harm to a neighbor; therefore love is the fulfillment of the law.*
>
> *(Romans 13:8-10)*

Taxes would be much lower as there would be no need for prisons, courts, judges, lawyers, etc. This would mean less working hours, because the cost of living would be lower and therefore families could spend more time together, giving security that is so necessary both to children and married couples. There would be little stress because people would rest on the Sabbath, and therefore no need for psychiatrists.

Blessing would be on the land, so the soil would bring forth fruit in its season. Pestilence would be removed (no more pesticides). God's blessing of health would be on the people, and so there would be little need for doctors, mental institutions and hospitals. AIDS, cancer, and other plagues would be a thing of the past.

God's commandments are more to be desired than gold; in keeping of them, there is great reward. How true is the Scripture, *"Blessed be the nation whose God is the LORD"* (Psalm 33:12).

Abraham Lincoln said of the United States:

> We have preserved these many years in peace and prosperity. We have grown in numbers, wealth and power as no other nation has ever grown...but we have forgotten God! We have forgotten the gracious Hand which preserved us in peace, and multiplied, and enriched, and strengthened us; and we have vainly imagined in the deceitfulness of our hearts, that all these blessings were produced by some superior wisdom and virtue of our own.

> Intoxicated with unbroken success, we have become too self-sufficient to feel the necessity of redeeming and preserving grace, too proud to pray to the God that made us!
>
> It behooves us then, to humble ourselves before the offended Power, to confess our national sins and pray for clemency and forgiveness.

Who knows, if this once great nation obeyed the command to repent, if Christians obeyed the edict to *"lift up your voice like a trumpet, [and] tell My people their transgression"* (Isaiah 58:1), God just may in His great mercy forgive our sins and heal this land.

The only way to satisfy the Sabbath law, and each of the commandments, is to be in Christ. Jesus kept the Sabbath holy. The Bible says He knew no sin, and therefore never once did He violate the Sabbath law in letter or in spirit. Never once did He complain, even in the depths of His soul, of the fact that the Sabbath was the day He ceased from all labor.

He who trusts in the Savior partakes in the blessings of His obedience. He then, through the work of the Holy Spirit, has the law written on his heart by the blood-stained ink of God's grace, and can say, "I am saved from the wrath of God's law."

Oh, that there were such a heart in them, that they would fear Me, and keep all My commandments always, that it might be well with them, and with their children forever. *(Deuteronomy 5:29)*

Chapter Six
Too Hot to Handle

Honor your father and mother.
—Exodus 20:12

I could hardly believe my eyes. I was reading about a man who so hated his father, he spat on his corpse as he leaned over the casket at his funeral. What on earth would cause a man, a professing Christian, to hate his own flesh and blood with such intensity? The answer is simply a lack of knowledge. His was a common story. His father was a drunk, who caused so many problems in his small home town, he was despised by the whole community. Unfortunately, as a child, the son bore hatred for the sins of his father, and his resentment towards him grew until it consumed him.

In fact, in my experience, one almost certain way to open yourself up to the demonic realm, is to violate the fifth commandment by hating your parents. The Bible warns, *"Honor your father and your mother, that your days may be long upon the land which the LORD your God is giving you"* (Exodus 20:12).

After hearing ministry about the necessity to forgive from the heart, the man gained knowledge and understood how unforgiveness was actually binding him, destroying his own life as well as the life of his family. On finding a place of repentance he said, "I feel like ten tons came off me. Right now I'm a new man!" Those "ten tons" were the weight of God's law upon his guilty soul. This "Christian" had just become a new creature in Christ. Paul said, *"The law brings about wrath"* (Romans 4:15), and that wrath abides on the sinner until he comes to the place of biblical repentance, despite his so-called profession of faith.

The commandment says, *"Honor your mother and father,"* which is totally unconditional. It doesn't say honor them **if** they are worthy. No parent is "worthy" in the sight of God. No one knows that better than me. I'm a parent, and I know that in me dwells no good thing, outside of the Savior. I know what I am, and I know that I am not worthy of the honor commanded by the law. When the Bible says **all** have sinned, it means all. There is none righteous, not one. The issue with the fifth commandment is not the worthiness of the parents, but the obedience of the children.

Once again, the law is without mercy towards those that transgress it and dishonor their parents:

> *If a man has a stubborn and rebellious son, who will not obey the voice of his father or the voice of his mother, and that, when they have chastened him, will not harken unto them, then shall his father and his mother lay hold on him, and bring him out unto the elders of his city, and unto the gate of his place. And they shall say unto the elders of his city, "This, our son, is stubborn and rebellious. He will not obey our voice; he is a glutton, and a drunkard." And all the men of his city shall stone him with stones, that he die. So shall thou put evil away from among you, and all Israel shall hear, and fear.*
>
> *(Deuteronomy 21:18-21)*

If the law were instigated within today's rebellious generation, few stones would gather any moss. There is no incident recorded in Scripture of a rebellious youth being stoned, but I'm sure, knowing what the law stated, parents were honored in Israel. In fact, Leviticus 19:3 KJV reveals our duty to parents to a greater degree by saying that we should even *"fear"* our father and mother.

Search the Old Testament high and low, and you will find comparatively few examples of dishonoring of parents. One incident was where Esau, at the age of 40 years, married Gentile wives *"which were a grief of mind to Isaac and Rebekah"* (Genesis 26:35). It would seem that the only other obvious occurrence, was when Ham, the son of Noah, looked upon Noah's nakedness (Genesis 9:22). When Ham dishonored his father, it was such a serious offense he came under a curse, which is consistent with harsh penalties for transgression, found in other Scriptures on the subject:

> ***Honor your father and mother,*** *which is the first commandment with a promise:* ***that all may be well with you and you may live long on the earth.***
>
> *(Ephesians 6:2-3, emphasis added)*

In other words, fail to honor your parents, and all will not be well with you, and your days will not be long on the earth.

In Matthew 15:4, Jesus said, *"For God commanded, saying, 'Honor your father and your mother'; and, 'He who curses father or mother, let him be put to death.'"*

Another example of transgression of the fifth commandment is given in the story of the prodigal son (Luke 15:11-32). Here was a young man who felt the fire of lust burning within his breast and preferred to honor his passion above his father. The respect he had for him was not deep enough to restrain the power of his own will to sin. His covetous heart drew him into sexual immorality. He had two obstacles that stood between him and the pathway of pleasure: his conscience and his father. Both symbolized the same thing—the law of God. He seared his conscience, which dealt with the law, and he moved to a far country, which dealt with his dad.

However, in the stillness of his heart, the Spirit of God stirred his conscience, to show him that His rebellion was not primarily against his father, but against his God. The work of the law was written upon his heart (Romans 2:15), his conscience bearing witness and accusing him of the sin of dishonoring his father. The extent of his immorality can be seen by his penitent confession, *"Father, I have sinned against heaven and in your sight, and am no longer worthy to be called your son"* (Luke 15:21).

The Pharisees were also guilty of transgressing this commandment. They dishonored their own parents, and vainly tried to conceal this sin by covering the commandment with the cloak of their tradition (Mark 7:1-13). The difference between the prodigal and his brother, was the revelation that sin is vertical, not horizontal, as the brother seemed to assume (Luke 15:29). This story was directed at these self-righteous religious leaders (Luke 15:3), who had little understanding of the true nature of sin, because they twisted the law to suit their sins. Their transgression of this commandment was even more wicked, because they dishonored their parents in the guise of honoring God.

Our honor of God should be so great that the honor and affection we have for our own parents should comparatively seem as hate (Luke 14:26). How many of us can say we have kept this commandment implicitly, never saying, doing, or even thinking a resentful or dishonorable thought towards our parents? If we fail to honor our parents in a way that's pleasing to God, how much more do we fail to honor God? Like the prodigal, our sin isn't against our parental authority, but against heaven. Until God gives us light, we honor our true father, the devil, and gladly do his will.

A generation ago, it was standard behavior to honor your parents. It was almost unheard of for a child to answer his parents back or show any disrespect.

The final words of the Old Testament show us the repercussions of a parent-dishonoring generation. In Malachi 4:4-6, the prophet reminds Israel of the law of Moses, then says that Elijah the prophet's ministry will be to reconcile fathers to children and children to fathers, *"lest I come and strike the earth with a curse."*

The relatively few incidents of parental dishonor in Scripture is a slap in the face of this parent-dishonoring generation. This age is characterized by *"disobedience to parents"* (2 Timothy 3:2).

Let us surmise that you think that you have kept this commandment: you have always honored your parents. You have fallen in other areas of the law—lust, a few white lies, you've 'lifted' a few small items here and there, but this one remains unbroken as far as you are concerned.

Let's now look at a nationally-known public figure. He is the mayor of a large city. He is respected within the entire nation as a man of integrity, a man of decent moral character. His parents are proud of him and have actually glowed with joy at his achievements as they were interviewed on television about their son being held in such high esteem.

One day the supermarket tabloids headline the name of the mayor, saying that he was arrested while frequenting a local brothel. Suddenly, the story moves from headline gossip to fact, as the man is charged, tried, and found guilty by the court system. What has happened? He has publicly disgraced the family name. He has dishonored his parents before the whole nation.

So, you have never dishonored your parents? You have however, by your own admission, lied, stolen and lusted. You are a thief, a liar and an adulterer at heart.

You are not a nationally-known figure, and therefore the public doesn't know about your shameful vices. Does their ignorance make you less guilty or more righteous than the well-known public figure? Your sins may not be known on earth, but they are certainly known in heaven!

As far as God is concerned, you have brought shame to your family name, you have miserably dishonored your parents, and even added to your sins with self-righteous boasting.

Laughing Gear

It was 100 degrees plus as I stepped off the plane in Arizona. The cool air of the terminal was like a breath of fresh air. To put it mildly, I don't like heat. I find it's a breeze to get hot if I'm cold, but it's not so easy to get cool if I'm hot.

My mind was taken off the temperature by the growlings of my stomach. It was two hours passed lunch time, so I decided to take in a beef taco.

I sat down and wrapped my laughing gear (down-under colloquialism) around a Mexican monster. Suddenly, my mouth was on fire! The "taco" was a hand grenade of hot sauce disguised as lunch! I had broken my first rule of Mexican edibles: check the sauce first. I swung the thing around to get a bite from the other end to put the fire out. It was then that I broke rule number two: never bite a soft beef taco at both ends in public. Now I found myself covered in red hot sauce, with a stampede of beef dripping onto my hands. It took a large chocolate chip cookie (any excuse) to give me my mouth back.

In her hunger for pleasure, America bit off a lot more than she could chew. The first bite came in the sexual revolution of the sixties. Penicillin meant that syphilis and other sexually transmitted diseases were now treatable, so the binding yoke of consequential restraint was removed to make way for "free love."

The heat started in the seventies. AIDS ignited in the eighties, and in the nineties the heat became unbearable. America's mistake became publicly evident to all. What was sown in the sixties was reaped as a whirlwind, less than a generation later. We are reaping the fruit of the lawless parent who found sexual liberty in the sixties, and so raised his child without the moral law.

America took the ten commandments off the walls and replaced the law with a condom. The child who is given sexual license will find that his restraint will be governed by pleasure, rather than a moral boundary. If he is left to be a law to himself, he will lie if it pleases him to do so. He will steal if he thinks he can escape justice. If he is not told *"Honor your father and mother,"* the unbridled liberty given to him will eventually backfire on the parents. When he oversteps what they consider the moral boundary, he will resent their attempts at restraint. The deadened conscience will allow hatred, until it becomes murder within his heart.

Three hundred children each year in the U.S. murder their parents, accounting for 2% of all homicides. One sixteen-year-old killed his father, after an argument about his continual absence from school. Before he killed him, he made the sign of the cross. He confessed on national television, "If I was to die today, I would go straight to hell." He received two days in jail and six months probation under man's law.

The June 8, 1992, issue of *Newsweek* said, "From ancient Greece to cold-war America, educators felt comfortable making absolute distinctions between right and wrong; family, church and school were considered a triangle of moral education, with each corner pulling equal weight."

What was the cornerstone of the values spoken of? It was the ten commandments. Now that the law has not only been forsaken, but so blatantly violated, *Newsweek* expresses the dilemma: "If you tell a community that you're going to teach values, some people go nuts...'What values? Whose values?'"

Sexual license has brought destruction to the fabric of our society. The strong and blind Samson of sexual sin has been allowed to push aside the pillars of the two tablets of the law, and the very structure of this once great nation has collapsed.

Adultery and marriage go together like a horse and a carriage full of hungry lions. As the sharp claws of the beasts rip into the back of the horse, it has upturned the carriage holding the precious children of the family unit. There is a direct correlation between disrupted homes and almost every other social evil.

According to Carl Zinsmeister, a scholar at the American Enterprise Institute, more than 80% of the adolescents in psychiatric hospitals come from broken families. Approximately three out of every four teenage suicides "occur in the households where a parent has been absent." A 1988 study by Douglas A. Smith and G. Roger Jaroura revealed that "the percentage of single-parent households with teenage children...is significantly associated with rates of violent crime and burglary." Another thirty-year longevity study tracked every child born on the island of Kauai after 1955, and found that "five out of every six delinquents who had an adult criminal record came from families where a parent was absent."

Those who violate traffic laws by 20 m.p.h. should not complain when a car speeds by them violating the law by 60 m.p.h. Pornography fans shouldn't complain about child pornography and the perversions associated with it. Neither should adulterers complain about homosexuals. He who steals time from his boss cannot condemn he who steals money from a bank. Those who hate their neighbors should not disapprove of anti-semitism or of the KKK. Open the can of iniquity wide and you have to deal with the worms, and worms we have.

Once again we see Jesus shine is all His glorious perfection under the penetrating spotlight of the law. He honored His mother and Joseph implicitly. Those that would point to the temple incident when, at the age of twelve, Jesus supposedly put His parents through unnecessary stress, would do well to give the incident some thought. They actually dishonored Him by presuming He was with his relatives. Finally, after two whole days they made inquiry and found He wasn't where they supposed He was. When they found Him, the Scriptures tell us, *"He continued in subjection to them"* (Luke 2:51 NAS).

Chapter Seven
The Wrong Door

You shall not murder. —*Exodus 20:13*

Recently, Thomas Lyndon Jr. of Rocky Point, Long Island, confessed to the murder of a woman during a robbery. He admitted that he held the point of a four-inch hunting knife to her throat, and then "dug it in a little deeper" after she awoke and tried to struggle.

He said that after Lea Greene stopped moving, "I counted her heartbeats out of curiosity to see how long it'd take her to die...I knew exactly what I was doing...I knew it was against the law...I felt powerful—invincible, sort of, you know?"

How true are the words of Charles Spurgeon: "Look at fallen human nature. Whitefield used to say that it was half beast and half devil. I question whether both beast and devil are not slandered by being compared with man when he is left to his own."

When a generation loses sight of God's law, it loses sight of the fear of God. That produces a man "left on his own." All he then needs is the opportunity, and the belief that civil law will not catch him, to carry out his heart's desire, including the taking of another's life.

Thinking I was almost alone in my advocation of the death penalty, I was surprised to see that 80% of those within the state of California actually believe in capital punishment. When the Bible says, *"an eye for an eye"* (Deuteronomy 19:21), it is speaking of just retribution through the judicial system. It is saying that if someone takes a life, they should pay for it with their life.

"Thou shalt not kill" is not, as some would try to say, inclusive of animals and therefore a confirmation for the lifestyle of vegetarianism. The Hebrew word translated in the KJV as *"kill"* is *ratsach.* It is a direct reference to murder.

The purpose of capital punishment is not primarily that of a deterrent. If one of my children lied, I would punish him, not because I want to deter the others, but because he did wrong. If the others are deterred because of the punishment, well and good, but that is not my primary objective.

Each day in the United States 95 people become gunshot victims. In a nation of 250 million, there were an incredible 200 million guns in circulation in 1992, with another 10,000 being sold each day. Every seventh person you pass on the street in America is carrying a weapon, either on their person or in their car. 1990 had just under 13,000 gun-related murders. At that rate, in just ten years 130,000 people will be murdered by guns in the U.S., not to mention how many more will have their lives taken from them by other means. Then add to the list the millions of murders of the unborn, whose blood cries out to God for vengeance. Murder is rampant in America.

We have come a long way since the first murder. When Abel's sacrifice was accepted by God and Cain's rejected, murder was in Cain's heart. The reason God rejected his offering, was because *"his works were evil"* (1 John 3:12). Further, we are told:

> *Cain was very angry, and his countenance fell. The LORD said to Cain, "Why are you angry? And why has your countenance fallen? If you do well, will you not be accepted? And if you do not do well, sin lies at the door. And its desire is for you, but you should rule over it."*
>
> *(Genesis 4:5-7)*

God gave him warning, and yet he still took the life of his brother. Murder is far more serious than most of us realize. When a man takes the life of another person, he also takes the life of his children and his children's children that now will never be. He actually cuts off a whole generation.

How true is the statement, *"Sin lies at the door."* Like a snarling and powerful tiger, it waits to leap from the human heart and devour all who resist its debased will. We hide sin well until someone scratches the surface. Anger and hatred boil over in racial tensions, marriage disputes, clashes between unions, sports teams, borders of countries, boundaries of neighbors, between police and criminals, between rival gangs, and political parties. God says of us:

> *Their feet are swift to shed blood; destruction and misery are in their ways; the way of peace they have not known. There is no fear of God before their eyes.*
>
> *(Romans 3:15-18)*

Human nature is disagreeable to say the least. In fact, I don't think two human beings can agree on any one point—and I'm sure you would agree with that statement!

We don't have to shed blood to be guilty of violating the law of God. Jesus warned:

> *You have heard that it was said to those of old, "You shall not murder," and whoever murders will be in danger of judgment. But I say to you that whoever is angry with his brother without cause shall be in*

danger of judgment. And whoever says to his brother, "Raca!" shall be in danger of the council. But whoever says, "You fool!" shall be in danger of hell fire.

(Matthew 5:21-22)

Once again, Jesus is telling us the spirit of the law and what it truly demands. The essence of the law is that we are to love our enemies, bless those that curse us, and do good to those who despitefully use us (Matthew 5:44). How far each of us fall short of God's criterion. We can hardly get along with those we call our "loved ones."

The world would do well to look back to the Scriptures as a structure for civil law. Often we hear the argument that innocent people may die if we instigate capital punishment. With the structure of the court system and with the way evidence is presented, this may well happen. The Bible says that only by *"the mouth of two or three witnesses"* (Numbers 35:30) shall a man be put to death. If there are no witnesses, merely circumstantial evidence, then life should be spared. God will get him on judgment day, if he is guilty.

Under biblical law, a guilty person was allowed to flee to a *"city of refuge."* He fled there because the *"avenger of blood"* chased him there. (See Numbers 35.) If there had been no avenger of blood, the guilty transgressor would have had no reason to seek a haven.

The law of God is the avenger of the blood of guilty sinners. It cries out for justice against condemned transgressors. Who of us can face that law and say, "I have never been angry without cause; I have never hated anybody"? Why, I have felt murder in my heart on the freeway when some poor person is going a little slower than me. *"If You, LORD, should mark iniquities, who could stand?"* (Psalm 130:3).

The Bible equates hatred with murder, saying, *"Whoever hates his brother, is a murderer, and you know that no murderer has eternal life abiding in him"* (1 John 3:15).

The law drives sinners to the city of refuge of Jesus Christ, that they might have strong consolation, who have fled for refuge to lay hold upon the hope set before them.

When Moses asked to see God's glory, God said that he couldn't look upon Him and live. But in His great goodness, God hid Moses in the cleft of a rock so that he could gaze upon the aftermath of His manifestation. God passed by the rock. Later, when Moses came down from the mountain, his face so glowed that the children of Israel had to put a veil over it, because they could not look at the face of Moses after he had looked at where God had been!

Those who come to the Savior, find refuge in the rock. On that day, when we stand before the glory of our Creator, we will be safe in Him. That includes murderers who repent. King David took the life of Uriah, Bathsheba's husband. God's grace forgave him. Moses killed an Egyptian. God forgave him and used him mightily, as He used no other man. Saul of Tarsus held the clothing of men who shed the blood of Stephen, the first Christian martyr. He had Christians persecuted to their death, yet the blood of the Savior was sufficient for his complete forgiveness.

Get the Right Door

During 1985, I stayed with a couple for just one day, which was rather unusual. Typically when I'm traveling on ministry, I am in one place for at least two or three days. However, I had only one meeting with this particular church, so it was just a matter of needing somewhere to change my clothes and rest for the afternoon.

After dinner, I sat down for a few minutes and then made my way to the hall door.I opened it and found myself confronting the young lady of the home as she stood in her underwear beside her bed! I had opened the wrong door! I have stayed in hundreds of homes and this was the first time anything like this had happened. The hallway and the bedroom doors were identical. Deep in thought before the meeting, I had inadvertently opened the wrong door. There was a deafening shriek, after which I pulled myself together, stopped screaming, and then apologized.

There are only two doors—the door to heaven and the door to hell. Without the law, both look identical from the outside. The Bible warns us:

> *There is a way that seems right to man,*
> *but the end thereof is the way of death.*
> *(Proverbs 14:12)*

Of all things in life to be sure of, it is that you have the right door: *"Make your calling and election sure"* (2 Peter 1:10). Jesus said, *"I am the door, if any man enter by Me, he shall be saved"* (John 10:9).

Jesus proved that He was free from sin—from anger and hatred, unforgiveness, bitterness and resentment when He hung on the cross and prayed for those who gave Him such a grim death, *"Father, forgive them, they know not what they do"* (Luke 23:34). Our transgression of this commandment gives God anger with great cause. The Savior is the only One who can face the law for us and take away the fierce wrath of Almighty God.

Chapter Eight

Sleeping At the Wheel

You shall not commit adultery.
—Exodus 20:14

It was spring. It was also the time when kings should have been with their troops. Not so with King David. God only knows what his thoughts were as he lay upon his bed that night. Perhaps he began to *"meditate within [his] heart on [his] bed, and be still"* (Psalm 4:4). Or perhaps he thought about his men as they arrayed for battle, far from the safety of his mansion. Maybe his thoughts were of God, in the beauty of His holiness. Maybe sexual passion burned within his mind. God knows.

Something that night caused him to walk alone on his roof. Something blinded his mind to reason. The Bible tells us, *"...and from the roof he saw a woman bathing, and the woman was very beautiful to behold"* (2 Samuel 11:3).

Little did David know that he was facing another Goliath. This one outsized the blasphemous Philistine giant. This Goliath was the subtle monster of lust. Instead of standing openly among the enemy and spewing out profanities, this giant took residence in his heart, and whispered as an angel of light, to the pleasure-loving mind of the flesh. Sin lay at the door.

As he looked at this woman, he was also facing another King Saul. This one cast the spear of unlawful desire at his heart. On this occasion David didn't have the quickness of mind to move from its piercing thrust. This time it was David who was losing his sanity.

The spirit of lust, like King Saul, would chase David like a dog, until he withdrew into the dark cave of sexual sin. Saul may have slain his thousands, David his ten thousands, but this blood-crazed spirit had slain millions of Adam's sons. David placed himself right in the path of its deadly course. This was the "*spirit who now works in the sons of disobedience*" (Ephesians 2:2).

David made inquiry as to who this woman was, and found that he had been eyeing a married woman—Bathsheba, the wife of Uriah. The king called for her. Perhaps he could comfort her while her husband was in battle. Whatever his reason for summoning her, the Bible says he "*took her, and she came to him, and he lay with her,...and she returned to her house"* (2 Samuel 11:4).

Sometime later, she sent a message to the king saying she was with child. How could he hide his sin? He called Uriah, Bathsheba's husband, back from battle and sent him home to his wife, no doubt trusting that he would do the normal thing and sleep with her. Not this soldier! He was so committed to the king's cause and to his comrades, he refused to enjoy the legitimate pleasures of marriage while his brethren suffered the hardships of war.

We are told in the next chapter of the depth of love Uriah had for his wife, yet this trooper here shows a commitment to his brethren which is hard for most of us to comprehend. Even when David made him drunk, he refused to go in to his wife.

The king had no choice; he had to remove Uriah. It was an easy thing to do. With the mere stroke of a pen, he had Uriah put in the heat of the battle knowing he would be killed.

When Bathsheba heard that her husband was dead, she had a time of mourning. After the time of bereavement had ended, David took her to himself and she became his wife. Brilliant. He had dealt with the problem with devilish cunning. It was neat, tidy, and swift. Like a ingenious cat-burglar, he backed away from the scene of the crime covering all evidence of his transgression.

However, the Scripture has ten simple and damning words for the King of Israel: *"But the thing that David had done displeased the LORD"* (2 Samuel 11:27).

Ten Simple Words

Maybe you have committed sexual sin. After all, "the majority of Americans (sixty-two percent) think that there's nothing morally wrong with the affairs they're having" (*The Day America Told the Truth*). Conceivably you avoided the pitfalls of causing an unwanted pregnancy; neither did you get caught. Perhaps it was just a one night stand, something you now regret. However, it's just something you did in the past, and as far as you are concerned it's gone, forgotten, swept under the neat and tidy carpet of antiquity.

But God has ten simple and damning words for you. They thunder their unbending commands from Mount Sinai's rugged slopes. Like David, the thing you have done *"has displeased the LORD."*

The Goliath in David's heart hadn't said like the Philistine, *"I will give your flesh to the birds of the air"* (1 Samuel 17:44), but that's what he did. The monster took the flesh of David's sinful nature and fed it to the *"birds"* of the demons of hell. David's affair cost him

God's blessing on his kingdom, the life of his newborn child, the peace of his family, and even the sexual pleasure of his wives. He saw the fruit of the *"iniquities of the fathers"* being visited on the children—God raised up adversity against David *"and his house."*

Sin promises pleasure but proves to be a thin coating of sugar on a bitter and deadly pill of pain. To get his unlawful desire, he had to walk through a mine field of God's law. He had to covet his neighbor's wife, steal her, live a lie, commit adultery, kill, dishonor his parents, put his own pleasure before God's will, as well as give *"great occasion for the enemies of the LORD to blaspheme,"* and then no doubt had to create a god to suit his sin. Nine of the ten commandments exploded directly beneath his feet, and one may well ask how David kept *"the Sabbath holy"* while in such a state.

Goliath struck David dumb with a blow to his understanding and cut his head off with the sword of his own sin. His act was without mind of the consequences. But it was also hard to understand, in that David already had wives of his own. Why would he, and how could he take another man's wife? It didn't make sense that the shepherd of Israel, the one who loved God with a passion, would walk headlong into the sin of adultery. There is a reason this happened, and it is the same reason why it still happens today.

Ever since I can remember, I have tried to catch the exact moment I fell asleep. As a child, I would lie awake at night and watch for the instant my eyelids dropped and I fell into the mystery of slumber. But each time, as much as I would determine that I would keep an eye on the process, I would find it was morning and I had missed the moment once again. In fact, never once in my entire lifetime have I seen the lids come down.

Up until recently, I would sit and watch a boring black-and-white movie on television and deliberately open my tired eyes wide to keep up with the story. Suddenly, Sue would say, "You went to sleep." It was an enigma, because I would never be aware of the eyes closing. One moment I was watching the movie, the next moment I was asleep.

Then it struck me—I was shutting down in the mind before I closed my eyes. The brain went to sleep a split second before the eyes dropped shut. The same thing happens on a computer. The terminal switches off a split second before the screen shuts down.

This is why so many people fall asleep at the wheel of their car. They are driving one moment, feeling a little sleepy, and the next second they are off the road. Why? Because they thought the sleep process was merely a matter of the eyes closing. They didn't understand that the operation involves a shutting down of the brain before the eyes close. They thought they were totally in control, and it was their last thought of this life.

I was once the assistant pastor to a man who was greatly used of God. This man had a friendship with his secretary that I thought was unwise. He ended up committing adultery, which had devastating consequences upon his wife and four daughters, not to mention his ministry and the local church. How could this happen? Couldn't he see that his sin would have such destructive repercussions? No. Like David, he thought he had everything in control, but his brain shut down just before his eyes closed. He fell asleep at the wheel. His understanding became darkened, and so, like a mindless blind man, he walked headlong into the hands of the enemy. This is why the Scriptures say, *"Whoever commits adultery with a woman lacks understanding"* (Proverbs 6:32).

God's testimony of us is not a good one. It paints a pathetic picture of our insatiable appetite for sin. The Word of God says of the godless, *"Having eyes full of adultery and that cannot cease from sin, beguiling unstable souls. They have a heart trained in covetous practices, and are accursed children"* (2 Peter 2:14).

Our adulterous eyes reflect the desires of our depraved minds. The popular movies are the sex-rated films. The sexually-soaked songs that fill the airwaves are only aired because they are popular. The list of sexually explicit diversity is endless: the soaps, pornographic telephone numbers, erotic videos, strip joints, massage parlors, brothels—these titillating obscenities stand as evidence that will damn those who reject God's mercy in the gospel.

Out-dated Law

It doesn't take too much probing to find that civil law had its foundation in the law of Moses. *"You shall not steal"* is the only one that has held firm. Civil law now gives the right to kill through abortion and smiles upon adultery. However, the state of New Hampshire recently voted to keep a 200-year-old law on the books that makes adultery a crime punishable by up to one year in jail. They did so to show that the state still cherishes some traditional values.

Being faithful to the one you married may seem trite, but God's Word warns that adulterers will not inherit the kingdom of God (1 Corinthians 6:9). The law shows the seriousness of the sin, *"The man who commits adultery with another man's wife, he who commits adultery with his neighbor's wife, the adulterer and the adulteress, shall surely be put to death"* (Leviticus 20:10).

In fact, the Scriptures tell us that if we as much as lust after a woman, we have already committed adultery in the heart (Matthew 5:27). How many women "dress to kill" to stir up lust within men! They are inciting breaking of the moral law and therefore are in transgression themselves. God requires *"truth in the inward parts"* (Psalm 51:6). He searches the mind, and knows the intent of the heart. Who of us can say we are guiltless, that we are pure of heart?

Sexual sin is almost always the top of the list of sins in Scripture. The law is not only against these, but *"any other thing that is contrary to sound doctrine"* (1 Timothy 1:10). This same portion of Holy Scripture tells us that fornication (premarital sex) is included in the commandment, *"You shall not commit adultery."*

The only biblical evidence that someone is a Christian is the fruit of the Spirit: *"love, joy, peace, longsuffering, kindness, goodness, faithfulness, gentleness, self-control—against such there is no law"* (Galatians 5:22-23). The law doesn't condemn these fruits because there is no law against them: they are a manifestation of God's holy nature.

So there are two laws, the law of sin and death, and the law of life in Christ Jesus. *"For he who sows to his flesh [through sexual sin including lust] will of the flesh reap corruption, but he who sows to the Spirit will of the Spirit reap life everlasting"* (Galatians 6:8).

Again, the function of the law is to condemn us, to shut us up in the prison of sin and death, so that we will accept the key of grace. If any commandment slams the door of condemnation and damns humanity, it is this holy commandment.

Chapter Nine
Ahab's Wrinkled Brow

You shall not steal. —Exodus 20:15

Ahab was a spoiled brat. He wanted something and when he couldn't have it, he went into a pity-party, fit for a king.

Ahab was the king of Samaria, and when he wanted to increase his estate by some area by purchasing Naboth's vineyard, Naboth reacted with, *"The LORD forbid that I should give the inheritance of my fathers to you!"* So the king went to his house *"sullen and displeased... lay down on his bed, and turned away his face, and would not eat"* (1 Kings 21:4). He ran to his room, slammed the door, and ripped the head off his teddy bear.

Enter Queen Jezebel. Her crafty eyes reflected thoughts so deep, they were drawn from the bowels of hell. Like an evil cat in the night, she stroked her lily-white hands and painted nails back and forth, as she caressed Ahab's wrinkled brow and listened to his sad story. Her sinister eyes narrowed as she hissed, *"You now exercise authority over Israel! Arise and eat food, and let your heart be cheerful; I will give you the vineyard of Naboth the Jezreelite"* (1 Kings 21:7). She drafted letters in the king's name and sent them to elders and nobles who were dwelling in the city of Naboth. She wrote, *"Proclaim a fast, and seat Naboth with high honor among the people; and seat two men, scoundrels before him to bear witness against him, saying, 'You have blasphemed God and the king.' Then take him out, and stone him, that he may die."* (1 Kings 21:9-10).

And that's just what happened. Ahab the brat got his vineyard. But God wasn't too happy with Ahab. He sent Elijah into what He called *"the vineyard of Naboth."* It may have changed hands, but God didn't see the new possessor as the new "owner." The Lord said to the prophet, *"You shall speak to him, saying, 'Thus says the LORD: Have you murdered and also taken possession?' And you shall speak to him, saying, 'Thus says the LORD: In the place where dogs licked the blood of Naboth, dogs shall lick your blood, even yours'"* (1 KIngs 21:19). That's just what happened to the cat-woman Jezebel. Dogs ripped into her flesh and devoured all but her hands, her head and her feet.

Then the Scriptures say, *"But there was no one like Ahab who sold himself to do wickedness in the sight of the LORD, because Jezebel his wife stirred him up. And he behaved very abominably in following idols"* (1 Kings 21:25-26).

Like David, Ahab didn't limit himself just to breaking the eighth commandment when he stole. First he coveted, then he became part of a lie, he was party to Naboth's murder, then gave himself to idols. God held him directly responsible for the shedding of his blood, because what Jezebel did, she did in his name.

When Adam sinned, he married you and me to a Jezebel. He made a covenant with the evil one. When we don't get our own way, the spirit of Jezebel is there to wipe our wrinkled brow. She only does what she does with our permission. When we *"give place to the devil"* (Ephesians 4:27), we hearken to her call. She *"calls herself a prophetess"* (Revelation 2:20), teaching and beguiling all who listen to her seductive voice. Her territory is the flesh; her vineyard is the world; and her master, the devil.

Thieves will not inherit the kingdom of God. Most of us think that God doesn't consider our stealing to be theft until He becomes impressed with the value of that which is stolen. I used to raid orchards as a child. We had plenty of apples at home, but I loved the excitement of the crime because I was a thief. He who takes a ball-point pen that belongs to someone else is as much a thief as he who steals a car. He who steals one car is as much a thief as he who steals ten cars. (Speaking of cars and theft—in the city of Los Angeles alone, an incredible 74,829 cars were stolen in 1992.) If you have stolen, and you are outside of Jesus Christ, then you are a thief and cannot enter the kingdom of God.

Notice that God said Ahab *"sold himself to do wickedness"* (1 Kings 21:25). The devil was called a thief by Jesus, who said, *"The thief does not come except to steal, and to kill, and to destroy"* (John 10:10). God only knows how many sinners have died in their sins, having beforehand sold their souls to the devil through theft. They steal what they want, and he steals what he wants—their very souls.

What unlawful treasure of this life could I hold against my soul, and say it was worth the loss of it to gain the contraband? *"What shall it profit a man, if he shall gain the whole world, and lose his own soul?"* (Mark 8:36).

The Christian doesn't steal. He obeys the admonition, *"Let him who stole, steal no more"* (Ephesians 4:28). When Matthew Henry, the famous Bible commentator, was robbed by thieves, he wrote the following in his personal diary:

> "Let me be thankful first, because I was never robbed before; second, because although they took my purse, they did not take my life; third, although they took my all, it was not much; and fourth, because it was I who was robbed, not I who robbed."

In March of 1993, a homeless couple in California found a wallet containing $2,400. Instead of taking what belonged to someone else, they gave the wallet to the police. It was claimed, but sadly, no reward was given. When the public heard the story, they showered gifts on the homeless couple, as a consolation for the fact that they were not rewarded.

The account made prime-time news a number of times, because people were astounded that they didn't take the money from the wallet. The remarkable nature of the story is testimony to the wicked heart of humanity. Here were two human beings who were actually honest. Wow!

We don't realize the eagerness with which sin crouches at the door of every human heart. Many, who would never consider themselves to be thieves, find sin rise up like a consuming beast when the door of opportunity opens. No doubt this was the case on May 14, 1993 in Chicago, when $600,000 fell out of an armored truck onto Interstate 55. Panic-stricken motorists screeched their cars to a halt and stuffed bills into their pockets. Motorcyclists were seen to cram their helmets with money and then speed off into the distance. Two paramedics handed the police $120,000. They only returned the cash because they thought it was "drug money" and somehow marked. $450,000 is still missing.

When we are tempted to steal, the spirit of Jezebel is there to encourage and even justify our unlawful act, whether it is tax evasion, stealing time from the boss, the actual "lifting" of an item, or failing to give God His due of our earnings (called *"robbing God"* in Malachi 3). The wrinkled brow of conscience is easily soothed by the soft hand of Jezebel. She made sure Ahab got his vineyard. She gave Judas his thirty pieces of silver, and she will give you the world, if you let her.

Chapter Ten
Let The Cock Crow

You shall not bear false witness against your neighbor.
—Exodus 20:16

The *Chicago Sun-Times* said, "The truth is—everyone lies!" This statement was borne out in the introduction of a publication entitled, *The Day America Told the Truth,* which said:

> Americans are making up their own rules, and their own laws. In effect, we're all making up our own moral codes. Only 13% of us believe in all of the ten commandments, and 40% of us believe in five of the ten commandments.
>
> We choose which laws of God we believe in. There is absolutely no moral consensus in this country as there was in the 1950s, when all our institutions

> commanded more respect. Today, there is very little respect for the law—for any kind of law.

The publication went on to say that their studies found that 91% of Americans lie regularly, saying, "The majority of Americans today (two out of every three) believe that there is nothing wrong with telling a lie. Only 31% of us believe that honesty is the best policy."

This statistic is reflected within our schools, as reported in *The Wall Street Journal*:

> "In the 1940s, about 20% of college students questioned anonymously admitted to cheating in high school. That percentage has soared to 75%."

Having a Loose Hand

Perhaps one of the touchiest subjects inside and outside of the church is the issue of giving. The Bible tells us God loves a cheerful giver. He sees the sacrifice of giving to His work on earth as a token of our love for Him. A giving heart also opens the doors of heaven to us in the area of God's blessing. We don't purchase it, we just rid ourselves of idolatry when we learn to hold onto the purse strings with a loose hand.

One man who put his money where his heart was, was a man called Joses. He sold some land and instead of keeping the money for his own use, he gave it to the church. (See Acts 4:36-37.) Joses' surname was Barnabas, which means "son of encouragement." His generosity no doubt encouraged the apostles.

In seems that Joses' benevolence stirred a man named Ananias and his wife Sapphira to also give to the work of the Lord. The couple sold a piece of land and gave part of the purchase as a gift to the Apostles. Ananias made a fatal mistake: he lied about the purchase price, and God struck him dead on the spot because of his sin. His wife, not knowing what had happened, entered the scene and also lied about the purchase price, and she instantly joined her husband in death. Heavy stuff.

God knows why they lied in the first place. Perhaps they gave merely to outgive Joses. Whatever the motive, it revealed that their understanding of the character of their Creator was darkened. Somehow, they either thought God didn't care about deceit, or that He was not around at that particular time.

Our God is a God of holiness. This is the same Supreme Being who warned Israel that no one outside of the Sons of Korath were to touch the Ark of the Covenant, lest he die. Someone touched the Ark, and—surprise!—he died. In the case of Ananias and Sapphira,

God's holiness spilled over and consumed the transgressors. He doesn't treat most of us according to our sins, but on this occasion, this husband and wife came to the end of God's patience.

We may not see anything too bad about a white lie, but God hates deceit of any color. He will not tolerate liars. The law condemns them, and hell awaits those who follow in the footsteps of the "father of lies."

In the story of Ananias and Sapphira, Peter's rhetoric speaks for itself. He asked Ananias about his deceit just before his decease: *"Ananias, why has satan filled your heart to lie to the Holy Spirit and keep back part of the price of the land for yourself?"* (Acts 5:3).

The man didn't get a chance to answer because it was the last thing he heard. He lied to man, but his sin was against God. He violated God's law, not man's. Civil law only frowns on lies under oath, while God's law requires truth in the inward parts.

The ninth commandment is ironclad in its demand. It is not like civil law that so often reeks of hypocrisy and inconsistency. For example, the law frowns on and calls for the punishment of a man who has sex with a minor. If a law-breaker seduced a seventeen year old, he deserves retribution. However, there is something magical about a woman's age. When she turns 18, then fornication becomes O.K. as far as the world is concerned. The chronological maturation of the female turned something that was bad into something that was acceptable. In God's Book, sex outside of marriage is iniquitous no matter what age the sinner, and lying is wrong, no matter what shade the lie is.

Lying comes easy to the sons of Adam. Whoever said, "Taking the easy path is what makes rivers and men crooked," spoke the truth. Most people lie because it is far easier than telling the truth. This is why Peter himself lied, when asked if he knew Jesus (Mark 14:66-72). The implications for telling the truth were fearful; he could smell murder in the air. It took the piercing sound of cock's crow to awaken him to his folly. May God awaken you and me to our sin. The first crow of the rooster should rouse us to the fact that we have sinned against God with our deceit. The second crow should cause it to dawn on us that on judgment day, every transgression will be punished. And the third crow of the rooster should be the realization that God's punishment for falsehood is utterly terrible.

Bob Vernon, when deputy chief of the Los Angeles Police Department, told a tragic story. He unfortunately witnessed the death of a five-year-old boy on a L.A. freeway. As he waited for the paramedics to arrive, he saw a woman coming up the side of the freeway calling, "Ronnie...Ronnie!" He stopped her where she was and told her not to go any further. She protested, "But I'm his mother!" He gently told her that her child was gone, to which she collapsed in a heap of overwhelming grief.

It turned out that Ronnie and his elder brother saw some boys across the freeway playing with a model plane. When they asked if they could carefully venture across, their mother said they were to wait until their father arrived home. He would take them across. Ronnie looked at his elder brother and said, "Gee, Mom doesn't want us to have any fun!"

The Bible says in Proverbs 1:8, *"My son, hear the instruction of your father, and do not forsake the law of your mother."* Parents warn children of freeways, not because they don't want their children to have fun, but because they care for them and want to keep them from tragedies such as the death of Ronnie.

The ignorant ignore God's law because it is obvious to them that God is the ultimate party-pooper. He forbids everything that humanity thirsts for: He says no sex out of marriage, He prohibits work on the Sabbath, He commands the restraining of appetites, He outlaws materialistic attitudes, forbids the convenience of white lies, and on and on.

In truth, the Bible says to keep off the freeway of sin. The vehicle of eternal justice is coming, and Jesus warned it will be so thorough, it will grind all those in its path to powder. The Scriptures are merely saying, "Wait until your Father gets here, He will take you to a place of eternal pleasure, a place where your eyes haven't seen anything, nor your imaginations have begun to dream of the wonderful things He has prepared for those that wait for Him and love Him."

His kingdom will come; His will will be done on earth as it is in heaven. He has new bodies waiting for those that trust Him—bodies that won't be subject to the sufferings of this life—no more disease, misery, grief, pain or death. Scripture promises *"pleasure forevermore"* to those that obey God, but it warns, *"All liars will have their part in the lake of fire"* (Revelation 21:8).

When the Bible speaks of Jesus Christ, the One who was the very embodiment of truth, it says:

> *You are fairer than the sons of men; grace is poured upon Your lips; therefore God has blessed You forever. Gird Your sword upon Your thigh, O Mighty One, with Your glory and Your majesty. And in Your majesty ride prosperously because of truth, humility, and righteousness.*
>
> *(Psalm 45:2-4)*

The King of Kings and the Lord of Lords loves righteousness and hates iniquity. His sharp two-edged sword is girded upon His holy thigh, waiting to come down upon all liars. He has loosed the fateful lightning of His terrible swift sword; His truth is marching on. Our only avenue of escape is to follow His example—be truthful about ourselves, in the light of God's law. That will produce true humility, which in turn will cause us to hunger and thirst after righteousness.

Chapter Eleven
Fifteen Minutes to Die

You shall not covet. —*Exodus 20:17*

If there is one sin that dresses itself in the guise of being less harmful than other sins, it is the cloak of covetousness. It is a brilliantly colored snake-skin which, like a soft garment, drapes itself around Adam's shoulders, promising security and pleasure, but instead, becomes a straight jacket and squeezes the life from his body.

Back in 1991, Americans spent $287 billion on gambling. God only knows how many families were destroyed and how many dreams turned into nightmares because of this subtle sin. It was Epictetus who said, "Fortify yourself with contentment, for this is an impregnable fortress."

Covetousness opens the flood-gate to sin. Before a man steals, he covets. Before he commits adultery, he covets. Covetousness can even lead to murder:

> "Seven percent of us say they would murder someone for money. That's about one in every fourteen people. Whether they could actually pull the trigger is another question, but 36 million of us would be willing to consider the offer."
> (*The Day America Told the Truth*)

In fact, covetousness was at the root of Adam's disobedience. Adam wanted. Think of how much human suffering would have been averted if Adam had replied to Eve, when tempted by his covetous eye, *"The LORD is my shepherd, I shall not want."*

I can't help but feel a measure of sympathy for Achan, because each of us could so easily slip into his shoes. Achan was the man who lived up to his name, which means "trouble": he "troubled" Israel. Joshua, chapter 7, tells of Israel's humiliating defeat at Ai. They not only lost thirty-six men in battle, but turned their backs on the enemy and fled. Joshua was devastated. He and the elders of Israel lay prostrate before the Ark of the Lord, until God told them the reason for Israel's lack of success in battle:

> *So the LORD said to Joshua: Get up! Why do you lie thus on your face? Israel has*

sinned, and they have also transgressed My covenant which I commanded them. For they have taken some of the accursed things, and have both stolen and deceived; and they have put it among their own stuff. Therefore the children of Israel could not stand before their enemies, because they have become doomed to destruction. Neither will I be with you anymore, unless you destroy the accursed from among you. (Joshua 7:10-12)

Achan was found to be the culprit. He didn't willingly confess his sin, but listen to what he said when he was confronted:

Indeed I have sinned against the LORD *God of Israel, and this is what I have done. When I saw among the spoils a beautiful Babylonian garment, two hundred shekels of silver, I coveted them and took them. And there they are, hidden in the earth in the midst of my tent, with the silver under it.* (Joshua 7:20-21)

Achan also wanted. He wanted, and it cost him his life and the life of his family, not to mention all that he had. They were stoned to death, and a great heap of boulders were heaped upon their bloody and bruised bodies in the valley of Achor. Covetousness destroys entire families. It is heavy and glittering gold, heaped onto the family boat until it sinks under its weight. It is a *"beautiful Babylonian garment"* which carries with it the leprous sting of death—it is a *"garment spotted by the flesh"* (Jude 23).

It takes about 15 minutes to be stoned to death. That's how long it took a Moslem Princess to die recently at the hands of those who found her guilty of committing adultery. The incident brings to us the sober reality of how harsh God's law is.

But we must remind ourselves that the law only reflects the seriousness of the sin: *"the strength of sin is the law"* (1 Corinthians 15:56). If a man receives a $5 fine from a judge, you may conclude that his crime was minor. But when a judge gives a man multiple life sentences, you may conclude his crime was heinous. Achan's sin produced in the Lord *"the fierceness of His anger,"* so the mere mortal mind must rethink its attitude to the sin.

Covetousness not only destroys individuals, it weakens the hands of the church. When the leadership put their eyes on mammon, they take their eyes off the Lord. When a church becomes introvert and spends its wealth on itself, it has lost sight of its purpose. It turns inward and lavishes luxuries on the lifeboat, and forgets the drowning multitude.

I find that the plague on the body of Christ on this earth, is that it is fleeing from the face of the enemy. The fear of man has *"melted the hearts of the people"* (Joshua 7:5). The enemy comes at us one way, and we flee ten ways. The lion is fleeing from the mouse. These things should not be so. Much of the church wants to reach the lost, but is bound by the accursed fear of rejection. Why? Because our priorities are wrong. We love our own comforts more than we love the lost. Some of us can find a measure of burden for unsaved loved ones. We pray for them with feeling, and plead with them to come to Christ, but our compassion hasn't depth enough to carry us into the world to warn the lost. We must root out the accursed thing that is *"hidden in the earth in the midst of our tent."*

The greatest safeguard against the sin of covetousness for any church and any individual is to keep a loose hand on the purse strings. Tight fists cut off the blood supply, as stated in the Bible:

> *There is one who makes himself rich, yet has nothing; and one who makes himself poor, yet has great riches. (Proverbs 13:7)*

A penny held close to the eye can blot out the whole of creation, and the love of money can blind the church as to the reason for its very existence. A dead man couldn't care less about the things of this world. The Christian loves not the world, nor the things in this world, because he died to it at the cross. Instead, the riches of this sinful world are merely a dunghill upon which he can stand to proclaim the Word of God.

I often tell the sad story of J.P. Getty. This man was so rich they couldn't even keep up with how much money he had, because it increased so quickly through the many investments he had around the world. Yet, this super-wealthy person installed a pay phone in his mansion for his guests to use. He had five unsuccessful marriages. When his grandson was kidnapped, he refused to pay the demanded ransom because he didn't believe it was a genuine kidnapping. When his grandson's ear was cut off and sent to the newspapers, Getty decided he had better do something, so he loaned his son the ransom at 4% interest.

The unsaved are blinded by covetousness. They choose the riches of this world, rather than the true riches. They store up treasure on earth where moth and rust corrupt, and thieves break in and steal. They are the blind being led by the blind. Their minds are continually being bombarded with sights and sounds to stir the monster of greed.

Advertising lives by covetousness. This year's model makes last year's car archaic. Cigarette advertising in particular gives credence to the fact that the fish are blind and brainless. The bait stinks, the hook is evident, and the water is stained with the blood of their own kind, but they are still lured by the same old line.

Who would believe that cigarettes could be sold with a smoke-screen of words like "fresh, clean, fun, laughter and cool"? Only those whose sense of taste and smell have expired could be duped. I can't believe how gullible the sons of Adam are. All the fat cats at the top need to do to get into smoker's wallets is produce a cigarette-smoking camel, or call their cigarette "slim," or "wide," and the fish go into a frenzy. The copious cats see coins in the mouth of every fish who gets hooked by their lies.

Brilliantly produced beer commercials make poison look sweet to the brainless. The sole agenda of the commercial world is to produce discontent, and their fishing-ground is the Ocean of Covetousness.

The devil literally offered Jesus the world. All He had to do was become a satan worshiper (Luke 4:5-8). Jesus resisted him by pointing to the essence of the law of God—the law He kept so perfectly.

This, the tenth commandment leaves the forever-desirous adamic race weighed in the balances and found wanting.

Chapter Twelve
From the Lips of Sinners

We have looked closely at the ten commandments in their capacity to alarm us and, therefore, show us our need of God's forgiveness. This is their God-given purpose (Romans 3:19-20, Romans 7:7, Romans 7:13, Galatians 3:24, 1 Timothy 1:8-9, Psalm 19:7). At the conclusion of each chapter, we have looked very briefly at the Savior to see how He measured up to the demands of the law. We found that His perfect and holy life completely satisfied a perfect and holy law. Let's now take the time to look a little closer at Jesus of Nazareth to see if He still measures up as we probe His unique life as revealed to us in Scripture.

At one point in time, the Bible tells us that the Pharisees sent out temple guards to arrest Jesus. They returned some time later, empty-handed. When questioned as to why they hadn't apprehended Him, their words expressed their experience. They merely said,

"Never has a man talked as this Man talks! No mere man has ever spoken as He speaks!" (John 7:46 AMP). No truer words have come from the lips of sinners.

No one spoke like Jesus. He said things like, *"I am the way, the truth and the life; no man comes to the Father but by Me"* (John 14:6). His words were without precedent. *"I am the bread of life, he who comes to Me shall never hunger, and he who believes on Me shall never thirst"* (John 6:35).

I am forever fascinated by the last words of those who have been able to utter their thoughts while on their deathbeds. It's in the face of death that many who have lived double lives are suddenly honest. It is on their deathbeds that men and women have spoken profound truth. Often the world would wait with great anticipation to hear the last words of famous people. Some, however, seemed to lack the great depth one would expect. A gentleman named Luther Burbank was said to utter, "I don't feel good," while Pancho Villa said, "Don't let it end like this. Tell them I said something."

Jesus of Nazareth's last words showed His command over life and death. He told His listeners, *"I have power to lay [My life] down and I have power to take it again"* (John 10:18). His last words dismissed His life: *"Father, into Your hands I commend My spirit"* (Luke 23:46).

He also said that He walked in sinless perfection: *"And He who sent Me is with Me. The Father has not left Me alone, for I always do those things that please Him"* (John 8:29).

He revealed His understanding of the law through His expository teaching of its spiritual demands. Therefore His statements about His perfection, in the light of His understanding, were either the epitomé of self-righteousness, or they were true. How could any man claim that everything he thought, said and did pleased a holy God? The difference was that this was not a mere man. This man was conceived by the Holy Spirit. His blood was not that of the adamic race.

He was either who He said He was—God in human form, without sin, destroyer of death, and the only One with the authority to give everlasting life—or He was the greatest egotist that ever lived. However, those who study closely the life of Jesus of Nazareth, can only come to the conclusion that this human being was the incarnation of the God who thundered the ten decrees from the jagged slopes of Mount Sinai.

If there is anything to show us how far we all fall short of the glorious ideal revealed in the law, it is the contrast between our unregenerate lives and the life of Jesus of Nazareth. This man walked in the law of the Lord. He was unique in that He had God's law written in His heart. The book of Psalms shows us this difference when it says of the Messiah:

> *Sacrifice and offering You did not desire; my ears You have opened; burnt offering and sin offering You did not require. Then I said, "Behold, I come; in the scroll of the book it is written of me. I delight to do Your will, O my God, and Your law is within my heart."* *(Psalm 40:6-9)*

His thoughts, His judgments, His actions, His appetites, His attitudes, His words, His life, always pleased the Father.

Jesus is the man mentioned in Psalm 1. He was blessed because He walked not in the counsel of the ungodly; nor did He stand in the way of sinners, or sit in the seat of the scornful. His delight was in the law of the LORD, and in His law He did meditate day and night. He was like a tree planted by rivers of water—His roots were deep into the ways of His Father.

He was not ignorant, as was the rest of humanity, because His ears were "opened." He loved the light and hated darkness. He drank in righteousness like water. He loved God with all His heart, mind, soul and strength; and He loved His neighbor as much as He loved Himself.

He was the Good Samaritan who stopped and picked us up, bathed our wounds, carried us, and covenanted to supply all our needs according to His riches in glory. He was a manifestation of love the Apostle Paul spoke of in his letter to the Corinthians. He was patient and kind, did not envy or parade Himself, was not puffed up, never behaved rudely, did not seek His own, was not easily provoked, thought no evil, did not rejoice in iniquity but rejoiced in the truth. All other things may fail, but Jesus the Christ, the Son of the Living God will not disappoint those who put their trust in Him. He is the anchor of the soul.

But He Was Different

For about four years, I put up with bitter opposition to the gospel from a man called Steve. Steve gave his heart to Jesus under the promise of happiness through the modern gospel, and when Jesus didn't do what the evangelist said He would, he turned from the faith and became a very bitter blasphemer. He would go to great lengths to discredit the Scriptures, and to publicly slur the name of Jesus.

One of his favorite arguments was to say that the problems of the world were directly attributable to God. If he purchased a product that proved to be dysfunctional, the problem was the responsibility of the manufacturer.

Since God was the manufacturer of the world with all its sin and sufferings, God was therefore to blame, not man.

Steve was entirely correct in the first part of his reasoning. However, man is not an inanimate object. We are rational, and free moral agents, and therefore responsible for our sinful actions.

This free moral agency is seen clearly in the life of Jesus. If He was just a perfect machine God had made, then He is not to be esteemed for such a perfectly holy and righteous lifestyle. Yet, the Bible says, *"Though He was a Son, yet He* ***learned*** *obedience"* (Hebrews 5:8, emphasis added). Therefore, He had the capacity to be disobedient, but chose God's will above His own. This fact is never seen more clearly than in the Garden of Gethsemane when He expressed, *"Not My will, but Yours be done"* (Luke 22:42). He had the capacity to rebel, but didn't. At any time He could have created a god to suit His sins, but didn't. He had the opportunity to lust, blaspheme, break the Sabbath, lie, covet and steal, yet He remained perfectly pure of heart. The Bible tells us He *"was in all points tempted as we are, yet without sin"* (Hebrews 4:15).

Every time you and I look at Jesus Christ, it is a rebuke to the natural inclinations and reasoning of the human heart. We think that it is obvious that Jesus would seek large crowds to minister the kingdom of God to, yet He went miles out of His way to speak to the sinful woman of Samaria. When it seemed naturally right to keep children away from Him while He was teaching, He said, *"Let the little children come to Me, and do not forbid them; for of such is the kingdom of heaven"* (Matthew 19:14). When our hearts would esteem the strong, the proud and those who are first, Jesus esteems the lowly, the humble and those who are last. We want the best seat; He takes the insignificant. We exalt the rich; He, the poor. When we would draw back from suffering mankind, He was said to be a man of sorrows, *"acquainted with grief."* While we think it is our right to hate our enemies, Jesus said to love them.

See Him through the pages of Scripture, asleep in the storm, such was His trust in God. Watch as this man speaks to death itself and extracts Lazarus and others from its cold grip. No, this was no ordinary man. Never did a man utter words like this man; never did a man do the things that this man did. This was God made manifest in the flesh, the Holy One of Israel.

Chapter Thirteen
Ten Needle-sharp Claws

In the fall of 1992, a storm suddenly broke out on the east coast of the United States during a major golf tournament. As the thunder rolled and lightning flashed, almost everybody ran to the safety of surrounding trees to shelter from the rain. For a number, it was a way that seemed right, but the end thereof was a tragic death. Lightning struck the trees during the storm, taking human life with it.

Lightning always strikes the tallest object. The worst place to go in a storm is to the "shelter" of a tree. The safest thing to do, is to get as close to the ground as possible.

The day is coming when the God of heaven manifests the lightning of His fury upon sinful humanity. The way that seems right is to shelter under the trees of self-righteousness, to live by the "Golden Rule." Yet who of us can say that we have kept it, and done to others as we would have them do to us? It is merely another way of expressing the demands of the law as stated in Matthew 7:12. It is saying, *"You shall love your neighbor as yourself"* (Matthew 22:39). Instead of standing as a friend, the Golden Rule will stand as an enemy on the day of wrath. We have not done to others as we would have them do to us. We have failed to keep that commandment. It will flash as fiery lightning down upon all who shelter under its trees.

The only safety is the place of lowliness. It is to trust in the Savior. The world may mock as the Christian kneels alone on the lowly ground under the soaking rains of the reproach of Christ, but they will see their fatal error on that day of judgment.

When we look at the sins of King David, we can see that the only real difference between him and us is that his sin has been made public through the pages of Holy Scripture. He followed his heart's desire and took another man's wife. In doing so, he transgressed the law and swept his sins under the carpet of self-delusion.

No doubt the flames in the eyes of Nathan the prophet were fueled by the blatant hypocrisy of the King of Israel. David's indignation against he who had taken *"another man's lamb"* rose to a point of the kingly decree of the death sentence. He strained at the gnat and swallowed the camel. As Paul said, *"You are inexcusable, O man, whoever you are who judge, for in whatever you judge another you condemn yourself; for you who judge practice the same things"* (Romans 2:1).

Sin is like body odor: we can detect it on others, but rarely on ourselves. Nathan, as a true and faithful witness, stood before the king and said, "You are the one!" He told the king that his life had become an offensive odor in the nostrils of a holy God. Had he not done so, and David had been allowed to continue in deception, he would have treasured up wrath, which would be revealed on the day of wrath.

Years ago, I picked up a cute, pure-white rabbit. I stroked it gently as I felt its soft coat against my neck. Suddenly, for no reason, it stiffened and dug its needle-sharp claws into my flesh, tearing its way for about three inches before I managed to get it off.

King David picked up the soft warm bunny of adultery and held it close to his beating breast. Now it had turned against him and ripped its needle-sharp claws in ten straight lines across his flesh. The ten commandments called for his blood.

David's sin had turned the ten cannons of the law towards his sinful face. Even though the Bible says that he had actually *"despised"* the Lord (2 Samuel 12:10), he had knowledge that the wick of God's grace had not yet burned to the full. He lifted his blood-stained hands and cried, *"I have sinned against the LORD!"* (2 Samuel 12:13). He didn't blame Bathsheba. Adam tried passing blame, but it didn't work. Instead, David put the responsibility where it lay and said:

> *Have mercy upon me, O God, according to Your lovingkindness blot out my transgressions. Wash me thoroughly from my iniquity, and cleanse me from my sin. For I acknowledge my transgressions, and my sin is ever before me. Against You, and You only have I sinned, and done this evil in Your sight.* *(Psalm 51:1-4)*

David found the place of mercy. When the law called for his blood, God the Father shed the blood of Another on his behalf, that David might be justified. One was coming Who would balance the scales of eternal justice.

As you and I look down the barrels of the ten commandments, what fools we would be to blame another, when the Holy Spirit stands before us and says, "You are the one! You have neatly pulled the carpet over your own sins until today. You are exposed, undone. The fuse has burned and almost disappeared from view. Every minute you wait brings you closer to damnation. The law has waited for you to turn, and it will not alter it course."

Someone has to surrender. Either you have to give up your sins, or God has to give up eternal justice. Don't hold your breath while waiting for God to become corrupt and pervert His holiness. His law is a reflection of His character. It is perfect, holy, just and good. As the woman caught in adultery waited for an answer from the Son of God, her fate hung between mercy and justice. One nod from Jesus and the wrath of the law would have shed her guilty blood, and justice would have been done.

The day will come when Jesus Christ will no longer hold back eternal justice. The great rocks of the law are crying out for your blood. If you are not sorry for your transgressions, He will let them take their holy and fearful course. Your only avenue is to follow the woman's example and hang your head in shame. Take the lowly place.

King David was justified because of the blood of the One who was to come. The woman could be forgiven, because Jesus was on His way to the cross to redeem her from the curse of the law. You also may be cleansed, made just, and forgiven of all your transgressions, as you look back on Calvary.

As Jesus hung upon the cross, the law fell upon the sinless One. All ten barrels released their full fury upon the Son of God. It was as though the Father enshrouded the cross in darkness for three hours, because the sight of the twisted, bloody, torn and writhing body of the Savior was too terrifying for creation to see. He became a curse for us.

His sacrificial death showed us the true nature of our Creator. The same unbending law that stoned the Sabbath-breaker, the adulterer, the rebellious son, the blasphemer, put Jesus on the cross. Every driving thrust of the hammer, as it struck the nails through the pure hands and holy feet of the Messiah, echoed out the ten holy decrees: "*You shall have no other gods before Me...You shall not make yourself an idol...You shall not take the name of the LORD your God in vain... Remember the Sabbath, to keep it holy...Honor your father and your mother...You shall not kill...You shall not commit adultery...You shall not steal...You shall not bear false witness... You shall not covet!*" Each drop of His sinless blood screamed, "This is my love for you, sons and daughters of Adam!"

> *He was despised and rejected by men, a man of sorrows and acquainted with grief. And we hid, as it were, our faces from Him; He was despised, and we did not esteem Him. Surely He has borne our griefs and carried our sorrows; Yet we esteemed Him stricken, smitten by God, and afflicted. But He was wounded for our transgressions, He was bruised for our iniquities...the LORD has laid on Him the iniquity of us all.* (Isaiah 53:3-6)

God made *"Him who knew no sin to be sin for us, that we might become the righteousness of God in Him"* (2 Corinthians 5:21). He commended His love towards us, in that, while we were still sinners, Christ died for us. His sacrifice was sufficient to appease the wrath of the law. It was not possible that death could hold Him. Had not the law been satisfied, the resurrection would not have taken place. The empty tomb means that the door of salvation has swung wide but low. All who humble themselves, repent and trust the Savior may now walk freely from the courtroom. The balance of the scales has been leveled. As guilty sinners repent and put their faith in the Savior, they are justified in the sight of God. They may now have *"boldness in the day of judgment"* (1 John 4:17), no longer facing the ten cannons of God's law.

> *Death is swallowed up in victory. O Death, where is your sting? O grave, where is your victory? The sting of death is sin, and the strength of sin is the law. But thanks be to God, who gives us the victory through our* LORD *Jesus Christ.*
>
> *(1 Corinthians 15:54-57)*

Now, all that remains for you to do is to obey the command to repent and put your faith in Jesus Christ. To delay is to rebel against that command. It is to despise such a wondrous sacrifice, the offer of mercy. To procrastinate is to spit in God's face, to trample the blood of the Savior into the dirt. To delay is to hold back your hand from the One reaching down to save you and say, "Let me think for a moment as to whether You are worthy of touching my hand." God may just lose patience with you. Humble your heart now, and say to your Creator:

> "God, be merciful to me, a sinner. Have mercy upon me, according to Your lovingkindness; according to the multitude of Your tender mercies, blot out my transgressions. Wash me thoroughly from my iniquity, and cleanse me from my sin. For I acknowledge my transgressions, and my sin is ever before me. Against You, You only, have I sinned, and done this evil in Your sight—that You may be found just when You speak, and blameless when You judge.
>
> "Create in me a clean heart, O God. I repent of all sin, and put my trust in the LORD Jesus Christ as my Savior. I will read Your Word daily and obey what I read.
>
> "In Jesus' name I pray, Amen."

The Finger of God

It is the day of judgment. The law has torn sinners from their graves, and now it is the *"great and terrible day of the LORD"* (Joel 2:31), when God will *"bring every work into judgment, including every secret thing, whether it is good or whether it is evil"* (Ecclesiastes 12:14). This is the day prophesied by Daniël, when he saw the Ancient of Days sitting in judgment upon sinful humanity. Daniel saw Him and said:

> *His garment was white as snow, and the hair of His head was like pure wool. His throne was a fiery flame, its wheels a burning fire. A fiery stream issued and came forth from before Him. A thousand thousands ministered to Him. Ten thousand times ten thousand stood before Him. The court was seated, and the books were opened.* (Daniel 7:9-10)

All humanity, small and great, stood before the great white throne of God. The sun so shone in the strength of Him who sat on it, heaven and earth fled away from His holy face, and there was found no place for them. No one could look upon the appearance of Him who sat upon the throne.

The books were opened. And another book was opened, which was the Book of Life, and the dead were judged, each according to their works, by the things which were written in the books. God was going to manifest the counsels of the heart.

Suddenly, angels lifted two of us from where we stood, and we found ourselves standing directly in front of the throne. Light from its midst shone right through us. I stood motionless, as the other man gave an account of himself to God.

I could hear confidence in his voice as he smiled, and spoke candidly of his faith in the Savior. He humbly expressed thanks to God for the opportunities he had had to serve Him, especially through the gifts of the Holy Spirit. He acknowledged that the ability he had to heal the sick, came from God, and God alone. He had also encouraged, and edified many through prophecy, seeing incredible deliverance of numerous people through the ministry of casting out demons. This man was no stranger to the name of Jesus; he had done many wonderful things in His name.

Suddenly, a deathly silence fell upon us. A finger came out from the middle of the radiant throne, and a voice thundered through the heavens, *"I never knew you; depart from Me, you who practice lawlessness!"* (Matthew 7:23).

This man's name was not in the Book of Life, and he would be cast into the lake of fire. Angels took him by his arms as he screamed,

"Lord, Lord!" and removed him away, out of our sight. This man thought he was saved, but wasn't. He had named the name of Christ, but never departed from lawlessness. He professed faith in Jesus Christ, but had lived in daily neglect of the ten commandments—he was a worker of lawlessness.

I now stood alone, unable to lift my eyes towards the throne of God. This was my day in court. It was then that I heard a hideous voice from behind me bellow, "The second death also awaits this one—he broke the law a multitude of times. He is as guilty as sin; let hell feed on his sinful flesh!"

It was the voice of the *"accuser of the brethren."* Somehow it had a familiar sound. This was the prosecutor, imploring the law to call for my blood.

Then another voice came from the right hand of the throne of God. It was the Word of God, and like a two-edged sword it flashed in dazzling light, and said, *"Who shall bring a charge against God's elect? It is God who justifies"* (Romans 8:33).

Satan cowered for a moment, then moved slowly in front of me, and pointed his bony and accusing finger right at my face, and howled, "Skin for skin! He broke the law! Where is justice? Where is the wrath of God?"

Then he quoted all of the ten commandments. Each commandment came as a fiery dart, but instead of cutting into my flesh, it bounced off the shield of faith which I had in my hand. The law should have made me tremble, but instead I felt great boldness in the day of judgment.

Despite the accusations of the prosecution, by the grace of God, I also felt an incredible sense of being pure in heart. As light from the throne became intense, I lifted up one hand to shield my eyes, when I caught a glimpse of the skin of my hand—it shone like the skin of Moses when he had been in the presence of God. Then the light which was previously unapproachable, seemed to part before my eyes.

Suddenly, I could see the face of God. An angel swooped down from beside the throne, and removed the shield from my hand. Faith had passed away, and I finally gazed at the One who spoke the universe into existence, the One from whose lips thundered the divine law on Mount Sinai. This was the Holy One of Israel, the very One who had fashioned my members. Tears rolled down my face, because I already knew Him! It was the face of Him I had known in the Spirit since my conversion. It was my Lord, my God, Abba Father, the lover of my soul.

Again the finger of God pointed toward us. Then He uttered His mighty voice and said, "This one is Mine, as it is written, *'They shall be Mine, says the* L*ORD of hosts.'* He has been saved by the grace of God, for the law of the Spirit of life in Christ Jesus has made him free from the law of sin and death. The righteous requirements of the law were fulfilled in him, and now this defendant has an Advocate in My presence, a Counsel for his defense—Jesus Christ, the Righteous. Guilty though he was, the blood of Jesus Christ, My Son, cleansed him from all sin. His transgressions against the law were cast into the sea of My forgetfulness. There is now no condemnation to those who are in Christ Jesus. He has been justified through faith. There are therefore no grounds for a trial. Case dismissed, through lack of evidence. His works follow him. Well done, you good and faithful servant, enter into the joy of your Lord."

I was once in the cold death-grip of the curse of the law. But the grace of God, one by one, pried the ten fingers of the ten commandments from my soul. The accuser of the brethren was cast down. As quickly as satan came, he disappeared. Because of Calvary, he had *"nothing in me"* (John 14:30).

Suddenly, before me stood a pure river of the waters of life. It was as clear as crystal, and proceeded from the throne of God and of the Lamb. The judgment had passed. There were incredible trees, and fruits, light, beauty, and unspeakable sights and sounds that my eyes had never seen, nor my ears heard, neither had these unspeakable pleasures entered into the deepest imaginations of my heart.

From the midst of the brilliant light came a voice which said:

> *"I am the Alpha and the Omega, the Beginning and the End, the First and the Last." Blessed are those who do His commandments, that they may have the right to the tree of life, and may enter through the gates into the city...and the Spirit and the bride say, "Come!" And let him who hears say, "Come!" And whoever desires, let him take the water of life freely.*
>
> *(Revelation 22:13-14, 17)*

Chapter Fourteen
How the Masters Did It

I have often wondered how Martin Luther, Finney, Spurgeon and other famous preachers of past centuries presented the law before grace. Did they go through the commandments one by one? To what degree did they cause trembling with the law before revealing grace? Fortunately, their writings and sermons have been preserved for us to learn how they did it.

Charles Finney said, "The moral law is designed to destroy self-righteousness and teach men their need of an atonement and a Savior. In short, God's law is obviously designed to declare the perfection of God and the total depravity of man."

Here now is part of Charles Finney's gospel presentation. Notice how grace is wrapped in the law, and how he shows sin to be the heinous thing that it is:

> "Oh sinner, why provoke your Maker? Your judgment does not linger and your

damnation does not slumber. When the law was broken and mankind was exposed to its fearful penalty, God offered justice to the universe and mercy for sinners, which He displayed in the atonement. To make this universal offer of pardon without justice would violate His law. A due regard for public interest forbade the Lawgiver to forgive and set aside the penalty without finding a way to secure obedience to the law. Therefore, His compassion for mankind and His regard for the law was so great that He was willing to suffer in the person of His Son, who became a substitute for the penalty of the law. This was the most stupendous exhibition of self-denial that was ever made: the Father giving His only begotten and beloved Son; the Son veiling the glories of His uncreated Godhead and becoming obedient unto death, even the death of the cross, that we may never die.

Now, if you are unrepentant, you have never obeyed your Maker. Every step you have taken has added to your crimes. When God has fanned your heaving lungs, you have breathed out your poisonous breath in rebellion against Him. How should God feel toward you? You have walked over the principles of righteousness with your unsanctified feet. You have lifted up your hands, filled with poisoned weapons, against the throne of the

> Almighty. You have spurned every principle of right, of love and of happiness. You are the enemy of God, the foe of man and a child of the devil in league with hell. Ought not God hate you with all His heart?
>
> Yet, in the midst of your rebellion He has borne with you. All this you have done, and He has kept silent. Dare you think that He will never reprove?

Notice Finney's deliberate refrain from consoling his hearer in his sins. In our ignorance, this is easy to do. Yet it is desire for his eternal well-being that is the catalyst for such action. The later the pardon comes from the Governor, the greater the appreciation.

Matthew Henry, the Bible commentator said:

> As that which is straight discovers that which is crooked, so there is no way of coming to that knowledge of sin which is necessary to repentance, but by comparing our hearts and lives with the law.
>
> Paul had a very quick and piercing judgment and yet never attained the right knowledge of indwelling sin till the Spirit by the law made it known to him. Though brought up at the feet of Gamaliel, a doctor of the law, though himself a strict observer of it, yet without the law. He had the letter of the law, but he had not the

spiritual meaning of it—the shell, but not the kernel. He had the law in his hand and in his head, but he had it not in his heart. But when the commandment came (not to his eyes only, but to his heart), sin revived, as the dust in a room rises when the sunshine is let into it. Paul then saw that in sin which he had never seen before—sin in its consequences, sin with death at the heels of it, sin and the curse entailed upon it. "The Spirit, by the commandment, convinced me that I was in a state of sin, and in a state of death because of sin." Of this excellent use is the law; it is a lamp and a light; it opens the eyes, prepares the way of the Lord.

Here now is Charles Spurgeon's presentation of the gospel:

> Lo, I see, the law given upon Mount Sinai. The very hill doth quake with fear. Lightnings and thunders are the attendants of those dreadful syllables which make the hearts of Israel to melt. Sinai seemeth altogether on the smoke. The Lord came from Paran, and the Holy One from Mount Sinai; "He came with ten thousands of his saints." Out of His mouth went a fiery law for them. It was a dread law even when it was given, and since then from that Mount of Sinai an awful lava of vengeance has run down, to

deluge, to destroy, to burn, and to consume the whole human race, if it had not been that Jesus Christ had stemmed its awful torrent and bidden its waves of fire be still. If you could see the world without Christ in it, simply under the law, you would see a world in ruins, a world with God's black seal put upon it, stamped and sealed for condemnation; you would see men, who, if they knew their condition, would have their hands on their loins and be groaning all their days—you would see men and women condemned, lost, and ruined; and in the uttermost regions you would see the pit that is digged for the wicked, into which the whole earth must have been cast if the law had its way, apart from the gospel of Jesus Christ our Redeemer.

Beloved, the law is a great deluge which would have drowned the world with worse than the water of Noah's flood; it is a great fire which would have burned the earth with a destruction worse than that which fell on Sodom; it is a stern angel with a sword, athirst for blood, and winged to slay; it is a great destroyer sweeping down the nations; it is the great messenger of God's vengeance sent into the world. Apart from the gospel of Jesus Christ, the law is nothing but the condemning voice of God thundering against mankind. "*Wherefore then serveth the law?"* (Galatians 3:19) seems a very natural question. Can the law be of any benefit to man? Can that Judge who puts on a black cap and condemns us all, this Lord Chief Justice law, can he help in salvation? Yes, he can; and you shall see how he does it, if God shall help us while we preach.

My hearer, does not the law of God convince you of sin? Under the hand of God's Spirit does it not make you feel that you have been guilty, that you deserve to be lost, that you have incurred the fierce anger of God? Look here; have you not broken these ten commandments; even in the letter, have you not broken them! Who is there among you who hath always honored his mother and father? Who is there among you who has always spoken the truth? Have we not sometimes borne false witness against our neighbors? Is there one person here who has not made unto himself another god, and loved himself, or his business, or his friends, more than he has Jehovah, the God of the whole earth? Which of you hath not coveted his neighbor's house, or his man-servant, or his ox, or his donkey? We are all guilty with regard to every letter of the law; we have all of us transgressed the commandments.

And if we really understood these commandments, and felt that they condemned us, they would have this useful influence on us of showing us our danger, and so leading us to fly to Christ. But, my hearers, does not this law condemn you, because if even if you should say you have not broken the letter of it, yet you have violated the spirit of it. What, though you have never killed, yet we are told, he that is angry with his brother is a murderer. As a negro said once, "Sir, I thought me no kill—me innocent there; but when I heard that he that hateth his brother is a murderer, then me cry guilty, for me have killed twenty men before breakfast very often, for I have been angry with many of them very often."

This law does not only mean what it says in words, but it has deep things hidden in its bowels. It says, *"Thou shalt not commit adultery,"* but it means as Jesus has it, *"He that looketh on a woman to lust after her hath committed adultery with her already in his heart."* It says, *"Thou shalt not take the name of the LORD thy God in vain."* It meaneth that we should reverence God in every place, and have His fear before our eyes, and should always pay respect unto His ordinances and evermore walk in His fear and love. My brethren, surely there is not one here so fool-hardy in self-righteousness as to say, "I am innocent." The spirit of the law condemns us. And this is its useful property; it humbles us, makes us know we are guilty, and so we are led to receive the Savior."

God used Martin Luther to bring great light to the church. Listen to what he said about preaching the gospel:

> It is right for a preacher of the gospel first, by a revelation of the law and of sin, to rebuke everything and make sin of everything that is not the living fruit of the Spirit and of faith in Christ, so that men may be led to know themselves and their own wretchedness, and become humble and ask for help.
>
> No one knows that lime has heat until he pours water upon it. Then the heat has occasion to show itself. The water did not create the heat in the lime, but it has made itself manifest. It is similar to the will of man and the law.
>
> *"I was alive without the law once: but when the commandment came, sin revived"* (Romans 7:9). So it is with the work-righteous and the proud unbelievers. Because they do not know the law of God, which is directed against them, it is impossible for them to know their sin. Therefore also they are not amenable to instruction. If they would know the law, they would also know their sin; and sin to which they are now dead would become alive in them.

Here's John Bunyan—writer of the great classic, *Pilgrim's Progress*—from his autobiography, *Grace Abounding to the Chief of Sinners*:

> In my preaching of the Word, I took special notice of this one thing, namely, that the Lord did lead me to begin where His Word begins with sinners; that is, to condemn all flesh, and to open and allege that the curse of God, by the law, doth belong to and lay hold on all men as they come into the world, because of sin.

Withholding Grace

A friend once told me how he was able to get an international Bible teacher to view a video he felt was very important. Realizing how busy the man was, he approached him and said, "It is vital that you see this video!" As the renowned minister put out his hand to take the video, the young man withdrew it so it was just out of his reach and said, "You have just got to see it!" Then he went to hand it to him again. As he reached for it a second time, he again withdrew it just a little, and said how good it was. Finally, when he let him have it, enough desire had been stirred for him to take time from his busy schedule to view the important video.

The well-known maxim, "You can lead a horse to water, but you can't make him drink" needs to be qualified. Although you can't make him drink, you can put salt on his tongue. All my friend did was put salt on the tongue of the preacher.

I often use this principle when I fly into a city to do meetings. I have noticed that if I get off the plane first, those meeting me politely say, "Ray, it's good to have you with us," etc. But if I take my time and get off last, they say something like, "Man, are we glad to see you! We thought you had missed the plane, and with all the advertizing we have done for the meeting, we almost died at the thought. It is great to see you...let me carry your bags!" In the same way, it is unwise to give a sinner grace before law. The law makes him yearn for and appreciate grace.

In *Lectures on Galatians*, Martin Luther said:

> Although the law disclosed and increases sin, it is still not against the promises of God but is, in fact, for them. For in its true and proper work and purpose it humbles a man and prepares him—if he uses the law correctly—to yearn and seek for grace.

It is truly to put "the cart before the horse," to give the sinner grace before law. Law creates desire. It makes the sinner cry out for the Savior. If you want hell-bound sinners to come to salvation, never give them grace if they have no knowledge of the law. Follow in the footsteps of the Savior, the Apostle Paul, the disciples, and the great men of God that were so used down through the ages. They knew that the biblical key to the door of the Savior is always "law to the proud, and grace to the humble," because God Himself, *"resists the proud, and gives grace to the humble"* (James 4:6).

Chapter Fifteen
Witnessing Using the Law

"Go therefore and make disciples of all nations,...teaching them to observe all things that I have commanded you."
—Matthew 28:19-20

It is the great responsibility of every Christian to share his faith in the Savior. We are commanded: *"Go into all the world and preach the gospel to every creature"* (Mark 16:15). In fact, we are to be ready to reach out to the lost. (See 1 Peter 3:15.) However, I rarely find it easy to swing from the natural things of life to the things of God. Something which has made it easier, though, is the use of gospel tracts.

Sue and I have published literally millions of tracts over the years, and the "I.Q. Cards" shown on the next few pages are by far the most effective for personal witnessing, if used correctly. Take the time to do the three tests.

TEST YOUR I.Q.

READ this sentence:

FINISHED FILES ARE THE RESULTS OF YEARS OF SCIENTIFIC STUDY COMBINED WITH THE EXPERIENCE OF YEARS.

Now count aloud the F's in the box. Count them only ONCE; **do not look back and count them again.** If you think you are right, look on the back.

There are six; if you found three, you are normal. Usually seven out of ten people get three "F's." If you found three, go back and check again. We have had people write to us and say, "There aren't six F's," and have had to send the card back with the "F's" circled. If you can't find them, write to us and we will circle the three "F's" you missed.

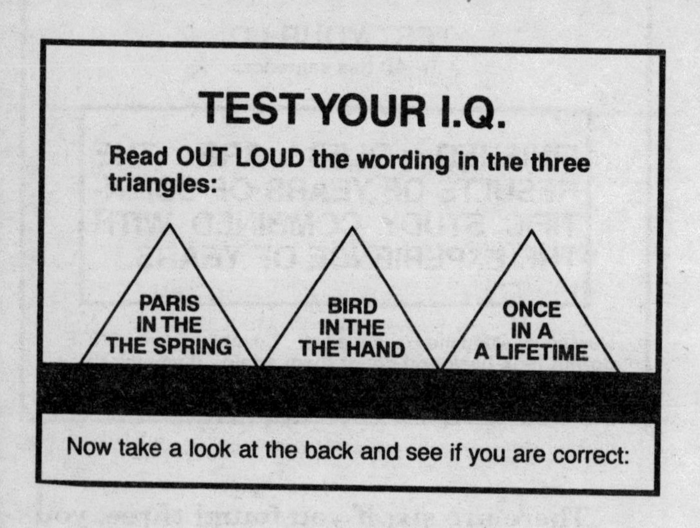

If you said, "Paris in the spring," "Bird in the hand," and "Once in a lifetime," you got three wrong. Try again.

(The words "the" and "a" are repeated. It's obvious, once you see it.)

Here is the third test:

TEST YOUR I.Q.

Add these numbers:

ONE THOUSAND
plus FORTY. Now add another
THOUSAND. Add TEN. A
THOUSAND more.
Add FORTY. Now add TEN more.
WHAT IS YOUR TOTAL?

Now take a look at the back and see if you are correct:

If you think the answer is 4,000, you did what most do. They mistakenly think 3,090 plus 10 is 4,000, when 3,090 plus 10 is actually 3,100.

Each of these tracts gives the answer on side two, then has the following:

Here is another I.Q. test. Answer "Yes" or "No" **Out Loud**:
1) Is there a God?
2) Does God care about right & wrong?
3) Are God's standards the same as ours?
4) Will God punish sin?
5) Is there a hell?
6) Do you avoid hell by living a good life?

The answers are, **1**) Yes. **2**) Yes. **3**) No. **4**) Yes. **5**) Yes. **6**) No.

You can't afford to be wrong! Find out the truth—ask God to forgive your sins, then trust Jesus Christ, who took your punishment by dying on the cross for you. Read the Bible daily and obey what you read. God will never let you down.

How to Use the Cards

Probably the most difficult thing about witnessing is bringing up the subject of the things of God. The card does that for you inoffensively. Another difficulty is knowing what to say. The card will help guide you through the gospel. Often people are self-confident and proud—the card will almost always humble them. Don't leave home without it.

Often you don't know if the person you are speaking to is trusting in grace or in self-righteousness. This card will find that out for you within two minutes of your meeting. In fact, it will also tell you the person's intimate beliefs about God, sin, hell and judgment.

Since I was converted in 1972, I have given out 50,000-60,000 tracts (not to the same person), and have experimented in ways to get them into the hands of the unsaved. I've found that there is an effective and inoffensive way to get strangers to take a tract.

Keep the cards in your wallet or purse. Then as you are getting one out, ask, "Did you get one of these?" You will have their attention since you are giving them something out of your wallet, which must have value. The question has a two-fold effect. It stimulates curiosity, as well as making them feel that they are missing out on something—which they have.

As they take it, they will usually ask, "One of what?" Smile and say, "It's an I.Q. test." Most people will also smile when they hear this (something to do with the human ego). It is so refreshing to have someone smile when given a tract. Many will try it straight away. As they read it, build a bridge by gently pointing out the object. If they fail the test, be sensitive that they may feel embarrassed when you point out their error. Take the opportunity to relate to them, saying that the majority fail it. Then say, "Now try the other side."

Don't worry if the person passes the test on side one. Just say, "You did well. Now try the other side—it's far more important."

So far you have had time to get to know the person (especially if they failed the test). Now comes the next benefit of this card. The majority of those who look at the second side begin to "play the game" and actually do what the card says. They read **out loud** the answers to the six questions on side two:

1) Is there a God? They say, "Yes" or "No."
2) Does God care about right and wrong? etc.

It is some consolation to know that in recent polls 96% of Americans believe in God; 82% believe in an afterlife, and approximately 60% believe in hell. So, few are offended by these questions.

When they answer out loud, you have an excellent opportunity to ask why they think such a thing, and thus get to witness to them.

When someone says they think God doesn't care about right and wrong, most can be reasoned with by appealing to civil law. Almost everyone thinks murderers should be punished, even if they can't agree on its form. Then say that if man, with all his evils cares about right and wrong, how much more will his Creator!

With this little card, in two or three minutes, you can build a bridge with a stranger, break down his confidence in his own judgments (eight out of ten times), find out his crucial beliefs, find out whether he is trusting in self-righteousness or grace, as well as witness to him, inoffensively. When he answers the six questions, you can say something such as:

> "You did well...you got four out of six correct. The ones you slipped up on were number three, when you said that God's standards are the same as ours. The Bible says, *'His way is perfect' 'Who shall ascend the hill of the LORD; He who has clean hands and a pure heart,' 'Blessed are the pure in heart.'"*

Learn the spirituality of the law. Study what they mean in the light of New Testament revelation. Digest the commandments so that you can go through them one by one, opening up each one to show that God requires truth in the inward parts.

Then, once you have clearly presented the law, say:

"And the other one you slipped up on was you said we avoid hell by living a good life. The Bible tells us, '*It is not by works of righteousness that He saved us, but according to His mercy*' (Titus 3:5)."

After you have thoroughly brought the knowledge of what sin is, using the law of God, uphold the cross in all its glory.

These cards are easy to distribute and extremely convenient (you can easily carry twenty in your wallet or purse). Feel free to copy or print your own version of these cards which are reproduced in the addendum. Just don't forget to put the answers and the second I. Q. test on the backs of the cards.

Plane Evangelism

I am often asked how I actually go about evangelism in personal witnessing, so for what it is worth, let me share with you a typical weekend in which I usually find myself flying across the country for ministry.

This particular day, I was about thirty minutes from our home at the ticket counter at John Wayne Airport in Orange County, California. As I opened my wallet, the man behind the counter noticed my I.D. (I have a head and shoulders picture of myself with the words

"Ray Comfort — Ambassador, Department of Eternal Affairs," and my address underneath.) He was impressed and asked, "Are you with the State Department?"

I said, "No, Department of Eternal Affairs...do you know the Lord?"

He immediately came under conviction and said, "No," pointed to the man next to him and said, "But he does!"

I said, "Eternal life comes from knowing God. Here, have this tract." I'm pleased to say he took it.

It is a great step for an atheist, agnostic or even a churched person to admit that they don't know the Lord. Most delude themselves that they know God, when they merely have a darkened understanding of Him. Who knows, those few words I spoke may have been a vital link in a chain of events the Lord has worked to bring that man to a knowledge of salvation.

I then put a few tracts on empty seats around the airport terminal, and proceeded to find my seat on the plane. The woman to my right was an African American, who was very responsive to my conversation with her. The man on my left was in his fifties and looked like a businessman. After a time of building a friendship with the woman, whose name was Debbie, I gave her the I.Q. cards, which she loved. She even passed the tests on side two, showing that she had a Christian background.

I felt that she wasn't walking with the Lord, so I gave her a copy of our book, *My Friends Are Dying!* (a book written specifically for the unsaved). I also took the time to write her name in the front of it.

Bill, the businessman, spent most of the flight either asleep or listening through earphones to the movie, so I settled for giving him a book. Much to my surprise, he was thrilled and almost shook my hand off.

Next stop was Chicago airport. I bought some gum and sat next to a man in his late thirties, asking as I took my seat, "Want some gum?"

He declined then said, "You're happy... why's that?"

I would have liked to say, "Because my name is written in heaven," but I preferred to first build a relationship with the man, so I said the first thing that came to mind. "Oh, I just bought some gum."

He mumbled something about me being easily kept happy. We then had a brief conversation about the fact that he was a scientist who had been to Europe, after which I gave him three different I.Q. cards. He failed all three, but was fascinated by them, so I did a bit of sleight-of-hand.

The lady behind him leaned forward and said, "How'd you do that? Do it again!" So I did, and gave her two cards, which she immediately shared with her husband.

It was then that I encouraged Steve the scientist to do side two of the test, which he failed, revealing his unsaved state, so I went through the law and into grace. Unfortunately, our boarding call was given, so I said I would love to send him a book I had written. He replied that if it was further to what we were talking about, he would love to receive it. He even asked for my phone number. We tried to sit together on the plane to continue the conversation, but it was a full flight.

I found myself sitting next to a lady who was an American who had been living for the last 16 years in my home country of New Zealand. Now that was a coincidence. We had much to talk about, including how our isolated nation was becoming more and more like the United States. She told me how she recently walked into a restroom and saw blood on the floor. Being a nurse, Sally called to the person behind the door and even pushed it slightly. Suddenly, a man wielding a knife pulled back the door, cursed her and rushed passed. There was a woman inside who had been beaten to a pulp by this complete stranger who had been hiding in the restroom. Sally called for help, informed the police, and the man was caught shortly afterwards.

Sally was obviously not a Christian, by the profanity she used while speaking to me. Once a relationship had been established, I did a little sleight-of-hand for her seven-year-old boy. She was as captivated as her boy, so I gave her the I.Q. tests. She did well with them, and as the flight was short, I swung from the natural to the spiritual by asking her to try side two. I was a little apprehensive because my mind (prejudiced by her profanities) had concluded that this woman would be an anti-Christian, women's liberation, pro-choice, save-the-whales person. Not so. She went to church regularly, and was very open to my reasoning about the futility of life. I spoke of the fact that death could take our loved ones at any time, making an obvious reference to her seven-year-old son. She was in total agreement. I told her that if she had entered the restroom fifteen minutes earlier, she could have been beaten by that man, or even killed, to which she said that she had often given that some thought.

She even nodded that she had sinned as we went through the law. As we landed, I gave her a Gospel of John and took her address to send her a copy of our book, *My Friends Are Dying!*

I often pray with people after we have spoken together, but this is usually not in the form of a "sinner's prayer." I would want to know that the person is in the latter stages of labor before I take on the responsibility of birth. Too many still-borns take place because of an insensitivity to the fact that the sinner must be born of the will of God, not of the will of the flesh. (See John 1:13.) As I have said, I see my responsibility as one of planting seed, and someone else will reap in due time. Now and then I reap, and enter into *"other men's labors"* (2 Corinthians 10:15). With the help of God, I am sowing the light of understanding, using the law, praying that God will grant repentance to the acknowledging of the truth.

When I flew back on the Monday morning, I found myself sitting next to another man in his late fifties, and earnestly prayed that he would be an atheist. We spoke for some length about the political climate and of our respective families. I told him I had three children, two boys and a cute daughter, saying, "Would you like to see a photo of my pride and joy?" He politely said he would. I opened my wallet and showed him a picture of a bottle of "Pride" cleaner and a smaller bottle of "Joy" household detergent. The man almost choked laughing. It's a good little ice-breaker.

When I gave him the I.Q. cards, he flunked all three. I was sympathetic and encouraged him to do side two. He answered the first question, "Is there a God?" with "No." Much to my delight, he turned out to be an atheist. I told him that I had prayed he would be an atheist. He didn't quite know how to take that. Then I took him through the "Atheist Test," which I previously published in *God Doesn't Believe in Atheists*. The examination proved to him that he wasn't an atheist at all. I could see his hands shaking with conviction. I asked him what building didn't have a builder, what painting didn't have a painter, and what car never had a maker.

Then we went through the law, picking out the commandments about lust, lies and theft. I didn't feel relaxed enough to go through all ten, because it was obvious that if Arnold had been sitting by the emergency door, he would have made a quick exit.

After speaking of sin and the fact that men deny God's existence because of guilt, I thanked him for listening to me. I find this is a good thing to do. It is similar to when a dentist is drilling your teeth. Given half a chance most of us just get up and run, but if he stops to say a kind word about being nearly finished or that you are "doing well" and "keep hanging in there," a sense of consolation (small though it may be) develops.

It was then that I showed him a sleight-of-hand card trick, where three cards are shown, then each one placed along-side one another on a flat surface. The ace looks like it is positioned to the right. When the person is asked to point to it and he indicates it's on the right, you pick up the middle card to reveal the ace. I asked Arnold the ex-atheist where he thought the ace was, and he pointed to the card on the right. I said, "Are you sure?" to which he replied, "Of course, I'm sure!" He was wrong again! Of course, I took opportunity to let him know that if we can be wrong with such a small thing, how tragic to say there is no God and be wrong on judgment day. I left Arnold with his thoughts.

After a time he pointed to a wreck of a house in a magazine he was reading and said, "You say every building has a builder. I wonder what the guy had in mind who built that!" It seemed that Arnold was telling me in a round-about-way that something had come from our talk. He even took a book I offered him.

At the stopover in the Chicago airport, I placed cards on the empty seats and felt good as I did so because I had just read in the paper of a Supreme Court ruling saying that it was a constitutional right for "religious literature" to be handed out at airports.

I then sat down and watched peoples' reaction to the cards. One boy picked it up and did the test out loud. He then read and answered correctly the questions about God, sin, and hell so loudly that people could clearly hear him 20 feet away.

After that, two clean-cut young men in their late teens sat in front of me. I asked the usual, "Did you get one of these?" passing them each a card. They both blew it, but were fascinated by the fact that their eyes could be so simply fooled. I did my ace card-trick and told one of them (Jason) to try side two. He flunked on two of the questions (numbers 3 and 6) so I quickly went through the commandments, emphasizing sexual transgressions. They were both very attentive. I had two books left and wanted to keep one for the person next to me on the plane, but when I asked Jason if he would like it, his friend Tony jumped in and said he wanted it, so I gave it to him and mailed one to Jason the next day.

On the plane, the man on my left flunked the test on side one. He answered side two correctly, but I was sure he wasn't walking with the Lord. He was very open and listened intently as I spoke to him of his responsibility and the fact that he owed it to his loved ones to lead them in the truth. He took the book and began reading it right there on the plane. The man on the right side of me was a Christian.

It is so wonderful to see the law do its work in the heart of the sinner. It is like a light shining in a dark place. I was once speaking to a Russian in a plane. When I asked him if he could name the commandments (77% of Americans can name at least three of the ten commandments), he said in a strong Russian accent, "You shall not kill...You shall not steal...You shall do no adultery." Then he paused for a while and said, "Don't blame God." If there were an eleventh commandment, that's not a bad choice.

There was no alarm that he had broken any, so I told him that God considered hatred to be the same thing as murder, and that no murderer would enter the kingdom of God. He looked sober and said, "So it's more serious than we thought!"

From there I explained why Jesus died on the cross, something he seemed to be able to understand. I then prayed with him, gave him a book and a Gospel of John. This was not a sinner's prayer, because I felt he wasn't at that point as yet. God will save him, in His time. We need not panic for fear that he could die before he is saved, if we believe that *"salvation is of the LORD"* (Jonah 2:9).

I once approached a young man who was using a string of profanities. After giving him the card, I did some sleight-of-hand to build a little rapport with him. Then I asked him to try the I.Q. test on side two. He said he had told a few white lies, "lifted" things here and there, and of course, lusted. When I gently said that God saw him as a lying, thieving adulterer at heart, he widened his eyes and used the name of Jesus in blasphemy, to which I replied, "And a blasphemer!" He looked horrified and exclaimed, "G-d!" I said, "Twice over!" He then put his hand on his mouth and muttered, "You make me feel like going to confession...I am so embarrassed!" Conscience did its duty. He didn't need a priest, he needed the Savior.

Remember that you are sowing in tears. You are planting seeds of truth from God's Word into the soil of men's hearts. Sometimes, this may only be a few words. When I saw a carpet-layer working in our church bookstore, I asked him if he laid much carpet for churches. I also asked him if he had a Christian background. He hadn't, so I told him the major reason I became a Christian was because I was guilty of lust, and Jesus said that to lust was to break the seventh commandment and commit adultery. He then said, "We're in big trouble!" That's the understatement of eternity. I know God is faithful to water that seed.

In early 1992, I was invited to speak at a church in Annapolis, Maryland. After arriving at the airport, I was picked up by the pastor and driven for about 30 minutes. As we slowed down outside a huge mansion, I said in jest, "I suppose this is where I'm staying?" The pastor said, "It is, actually."

It turned out to be the 10,000 square foot home of a Christian family. It was a weekend I will never forget—their swimming pool was bigger than our house!

The first time they came to visit us in our 800 square foot mansion in California, I told my family not to be at all embarrassed when I greeted them by kissing their feet.

Two minutes after these friends left our house, Sue noticed a woman standing on our driveway, looking very bewildered. When I went outside and said, "Can I help you?" she asked if my name was Ray. I told her it was, and she started weeping, holding out a tract to show me. As she did so she said, "These people in a grey van gave me this...and I don't know what to do!" She then opened the tract to reveal a crisp $50 bill and said, "I have never had anything like this happen to me before; should I give it to you?"

I told her that the money was a gift to her, and asked her if she had had a Christian background. She wasn't a Christian, so I said, "Well, it looks like God wants to let you know that you need to repent and get things right with Him."

At this point of time she was weeping, and although she seemed to have an understanding of God's personal concern for her, she had no knowledge of sin. If I had prayed with her at this point, she would have made a commitment out of an emotional response, rather than godly sorrow. So, I said, "The thing that helped me understand why I needed to get right with God revolved around my comprehension of the ten commandments. How many can you name?" She actually named six of the ten, so I reminded her of the four she had missed and opened up the spirituality of the law.

Then, like the woman at the well, she digressed off the subject and shared a little of the trials she had been going through. It gave me opportunity to say how sometimes it takes the death of a loved one, financial collapse and other problems to bring us to our knees so that we will listen to what God wants to say to us. I asked whether she would be innocent or guilty on the day of judgment. If God judged her by the law, would she go to heaven or hell? She said with tears in her eyes and a touch of justified fear in her tone, "Hell...I've been worried about that." Did she understand why Jesus died on the cross? She did, so I took the time to try and show what incredible love it was to suffer in our place. When I asked her if she wanted to pray and give her life to God, she said she was about to ask me if she could, so I prayed with her and gave her a Bible.

Thank God for rich Christians who have a loose hand. Money can be such a blessing if it is used the way my friends used it. When they sowed, they showed that their love was deeper than a five-cent tract.

These are just a few incidents of how I share my faith using the law. You may do it differently—whatever comes comfortably for you.

For many years I stood on the front lines of battle with the feather duster of modern evangelism in my frustrated hand. But in 1982, as I began to understand why God gave His law, it was as though He said to me, "What are you doing? '*The weapons of our warfare are not carnal, but mighty, to the pulling down of strongholds.*' Here are ten great cannons."

God resists the proud, but gives grace to the humble. The word *resist* is a military term which in the Greek means that "God arrays Himself as in battle." The ten commandments are His mighty weapons.

As I laid down my futile efforts and turned those ten cannons of God's law upon my listeners, no longer did they mock the gospel. Instead, their faces turned pale. They lifted up their hands and said, "I surrender all to Jesus...all to Him I freely give." They came across to the winning side, never to become deserters.

Chapter Sixteen

The Jesus Satisfies *Gospel*

Perhaps you have come to understand how the ten commandments are used in evangelism, but now you are wondering what your attitude, as a Christian, should be to the law. *"Christ is the end of the law for righteousness"* (Romans 10:4), but the regenerate person will not live in violation of the commandments. The reality of his conversion will be seen in lawful conduct. He is *"dead to the law by the body of Christ"* (Romans 7:4), but as he abides in Christ, he fulfills its righteous requirements.

Let me put it this way. If a certain object moves at a certain speed, it can supersede the law of gravity. A plane, weighing literally hundreds of tons can actually move through the sky as if it was weightless. The law of gravity still remains, but the plane is governed by a higher principle, the law of aerodynamics. If the plane in some way violates the law of aerodynamics, it will consequently find itself subject to the law of gravity and plummet to the ground.

In the same way, the Christian lives by another law—the law of life in Christ Jesus has made him *"free from the law of sin and death"* (Romans 8:2). As long as he remains in Christ, he is safe from the wrath of the law of God. If he violates the law of life in Christ Jesus and begins to *"live according the flesh"* (Romans 8:13), he shall die. He will be found to be a law-breaker with the great multitude of workers of iniquity who called Jesus *"Lord,"* but refused the yoke of His Lordship (Matthew 7:23, 21).

Perhaps the greatest error of the church of the 20th century has been to forsake the use of the law in its capacity to act as a schoolmaster to bring sinners to Christ. Instead, it has offered the gospel as a life-enhancement, saying that Jesus gives lasting peace and true happiness to all who come to Him. The message became that each of us has a "God-shaped vacuum" within us which we try to fill through drugs, sports, alcohol, sex, materialism, etc., but the only thing that will truly satisfy us is Jesus.

While peace and joy are legitimate fruits of salvation, I don't see that it is scripturally legitimate to use these fruits as a drawing-card for salvation. The tragic results of this method is seen in the massive rate of what are commonly called "backsliders," who are in truth false converts, and also in the moral and spiritual state of the church. Attracted to the promise of true peace and happiness, the sinner comes experimentally to see if Jesus is better than drugs, sex, etc., rather than to flee from the wrath to come. Tragically, when he comes under the promised temptation, tribulation and persecution, he falls away, becoming disillusioned and often bitter from his experience. His motive was erroneous.

Well Spoken

"But," some may say, "What about the adulterous woman Jesus met at the well, in John, chapter four? Jesus said, '*Whoever drinks of this water shall thirst again; but whoever drinks of the water I shall give him, shall never thirst.*' Isn't He saying that He can satisfy her thirst for satisfaction in life?"

If He is, then the reason people respond to the gospel is irrelevant. If Jesus is promising peace, lasting fulfillment and true happiness, then there is no better justification to say that it is a legitimate way to witness. So our message and the theme of modern evangelism should indeed be that Jesus can quench the deepest thirst by giving peace that passes all understanding, joy unspeakable, true fulfillment, and genuine lasting happiness.

Let's take a closer look at what Jesus said about this *"thirst,"* something He spoke of a number of times. He said:

> *He that comes to Me shall never hunger, and he that believes on Me shall never thirst.* (John 6:35)

He also cried on the day of the feast:

> *If any man thirst, let him come to me and drink...* (John 7:37)

What should this hunger and thirst be for? Is it for true happiness? Scripture gives the answer: *"Blessed are they who hunger and thirst for* ***righteousness****, for they shall be filled"* (Matthew 5:6, emphasis added).

Jesus' ministry was solely to *"the lost sheep of the house of Israel"* (Matthew 15:24), those who were under the law. It left them without righteousness in the sight of a Holy Creator. Jesus *"magnified the law and made it honorable"* (Isaiah 42:21). He brought correction to the perversions of Pharisaic interpretation by telling the multitudes that unless their righteousness exceeded that of the scribes and Pharisees, they would in no way enter heaven.

(See Matthew 5:20.) If they had no desire for an even greater righteousness, they would stay in their sins and therefore perish. He told them to seek first the kingdom of God and His righteousness before anything else (Matthew 6:33). Scripture tells us that it is righteousness that delivers from death; that it is righteousness which *"tends to life"* (Proverbs 11:19), and even likens righteousness to a *"mighty stream"* (Amos 5:24). Jesus Christ satisfies those who hunger and thirst for righteousness. The water He gives is in them a well of water, springing up into everlasting life. The Amplified Bible says in Matthew 5:6, *"Blessed and fortunate... are those who hunger and thirst for righteousness (uprightness and right standing with God), for they shall be completely satisfied!"*

When Jesus said, *"Come unto Me all you that labor and are heavy laden, and I will give you rest"* (Matthew 11:28), He was speaking of ceasing from our labor under the law, and entering into the "rest" of faith in His finished work on the cross.

We have been so soaked in the modern mentality that Jesus makes you happy, we immediately insinuate that He is saying to the woman that if she comes to Him, she will never thirst after happiness again. This insinuation also comes because we don't esteem and delight in righteousness as God does. We tend to gravitate more to pleasure than virtue.

If we study the passage carefully, we see that in verses 16-18 Jesus showed the woman that she was living in adultery. He put His holy finger on the woman's sin, the breaking of the seventh commandment.

It is true that God wants to bless the sinner. However, God's idea and our idea of what blessing is may not be the same thing:

> *Unto you first God, having raised up His Servant Jesus, sent Him* ***to bless you, in turning away every one of you from his iniquities.*** *(Acts 3:26, emphasis added)*

The blessed state for the godly is to have their sins forgiven and righteousness imputed. The very purpose of His incarnation was to give us the righteousness that the law demanded (2 Corinthians 5:21). Jesus died on the cross so that the "*righteous requirements of the law might be fulfilled in us*" (Romans 8:4).

To some, this issue may not seem to be very significant. However, to those who see the damage done within the body (with masses of false converts who think they're saved when they are not), and without the body (those who have departed from the faith—literally millions of "backsliders"), it is of great relevance.

I was once washing dishes and carelessly picked up a handful of knives. Unfortunately, a large carving knife for some reason caught on something on the counter, and to my horror, three of my fingers slid along its sharp blade and sliced deeply into my flesh. Those who handle the sharp two-edged sword of the Word of God with little thought as to the implications of their actions, sincere though they may be, do great damage to the body of Christ. They cut to the very heart of the evangelical enterprise. I think it is best to handle the Word of God with great carefulness, rightly dividing the Word of Truth, lest we end up with the blood of the ungodly on our hands.

God-shaped Vacuum

The thought that every person is born into this world with a God-shaped vacuum within their heart does have some truth. However, the phrase "God-shaped vacuum" is so much a part of modern evangelism's appeal that it is almost impossible to separate it from the thought that "humanity tries to fill the emptiness with drugs, sex, alcohol, etc." This conveys the disgraceful message that Jesus is better than sex and drugs, giving the sinner the wrong motive for coming to Christ—one of experimentation in the area of his own worldly well-being—rather than fleeing from the wrath to come because of his need for righteousness in the sight of God.

A sincere pastor once shared this thought with me:

> Up until 1946, sinners came to Christ out of guilt. Those born after that year are now "Yuppies," who have tried everything, leaving their lives in a mess.

He was adamant that the Yuppie generation will never be reached with the "guilt" message, saying they need to be told that the reason they've messed up is because they have violated God's law.

It may be true that the reason many are in a mess is because they have transgressed the law, but that message still communicates the erroneous "Jesus will fix your problems." The reason we come to the Savior should be because of guilt. We are as guilty as sin. The woman at the well had breached the seventh commandment. The reason she needed a Savior wasn't so that she could live a happier life, but because she was heading for hell for her adulteries.

The prerequisite for coming to the Savior is to have a *"thirst."* Jesus said, *"If any man thirst, let him come to Me,"* but it's not in the heart of the ungodly to desire Him. *"There is no beauty in Him that we should desire Him"* (Isaiah 53:2). *"There is none that seeks after God"* (Romans 3:11). The only thing we thirst for is iniquity; we hate God without cause; we love darkness rather than light. What is it then that makes us thirst for the things of God? I suggest that it's the law. The night before my conversion, I had no desire for righteousness. In fact, the word "*righteousness*" had as much attraction to me as the word "soap" does to a four-year-old boy. But the following night, when I understood that God required truth in the inward parts, I realized that without righteousness I would be found guilty, undone, on the day of judgment and would therefore end up in hell. Suddenly, the "soap" became attractive. I began to thirst for righteousness as a dying man thirsts for water in a desert.

Listen again to Charles Hadden Spurgeon speak on the function of the law:

> The law also shows us our great need —our need of cleansing, cleansing with the water and the blood. It discovers to us our filthiness, and this naturally leads us to feel that we must be washed from it if we are ever to draw near to God. So the law drives us to accept of Christ as the only Person who can cleanse us, and make us fit to stand within the veil in the presence of the Most High.
>
> The law is the surgeon's knife that cuts out the proud flesh that the wound may heal. The law by itself only sweeps and raises the dust, but the gospel

sprinkles clean water upon the dust, and all is well in the chamber of the soul. The law kills, the gospel makes alive; the law strips, and then Jesus Christ comes in and robes the soul in beauty and glory. All the commandments, and all the types direct us to Christ, if we will but heed their evident intent.

The law is like the burning sun *"which is like a bridegroom coming out of his chamber, and rejoices as a strong man to run a race. Its going forth is from the end of heaven, and its circuit to the ends of it: and there is nothing hidden from its heat"* (Psalm 19:5-6). It burns its heat upon the flesh of the weary traveller, driving him to the wells of salvation (verse 7).

In reference to the wells of salvation, Isaiah 55:1 speaks of a *"thirst"* within the unregenerate heart. Again, I would suggest that this is a reference to righteousness rather than happiness. In fact, the whole passage is sandwiched in between allusions to righteousness (Isaiah 54:14, 17; Isaiah 56:1).

If the promise of the gospel is one of true happiness, as modern preachers would have us believe, then for some unknown reason it hasn't delivered the goods for a whole multitude. This is evidenced in the literal millions of those whom we refer to as "backsliders," many of whom are still seeking the happiness they were promised, but haven't found.

Why not use the fact that Christians have a full and happy life to draw people to the Savior? The answer is clear. It is not biblical. Nowhere in Scripture do you find Jesus, Paul, or any of the disciples telling people that Jesus will make them happy. But what about the *"abundant life"* Jesus said He had come to bring? True, the Christian life is full. Study the life of Paul and see if he was bored while being stoned, ship-wrecked, beaten and whipped. Check out what happened to the disciples when persecution hit. Read *Foxes Book of Martyrs*, or study the life of John Wesley and see a man with a mission. He took the Great Commission seriously, and was always abounding in the work of the Lord, knowing that his labor was not in vain.

But, doesn't the Bible say, *"Happy is the people whose God is the LORD"* (Psalm 144:15)? Yes, and of course it is true. When a nation obeys the ten commandments, then there is no theft, lying, murder, greed, lust, etc. In fact, the first of the ten commandments sets the stage for the rest. It begins with the words, *"I am the LORD your God."* When a people have God as their Lord, they are happy—as happened with Israel under Solomon. But when there are Christians in a nation whose God is not the Lord, there will be persecution, if they are living *"godly in Christ Jesus"* (2 Timothy 3:12).

Christians who are in ignorance as to biblical evangelism will be drawn into the unscriptural methods of modern evangelism, as I was for many years.

How to Relate to the Unsaved

In our book *Hell's Best Kept Secret,* I have given the RCCR principle of witnessing, based on the discourse Jesus had with the woman at the well (John 4:1). These are the four principles: Relate, Create, Convict, Reveal. Jesus related to the woman, in the natural realm (John 4:7). Then He created opportunity to speak about the things of God, with a deliberate swing from the natural to the spiritual (verse 10). From there, He brought conviction of sin using the law (verses 16-18), and finally, He revealed Himself to her as the Messiah (verse 26).

After many years of relating to sinners, in an effort to witness to them (speaking about the weather, sports, etc.), I have found the most effective way for me to do this, is to use the I.Q. cards mentioned in this book.

Another excellent way to witness is to use our pennies, which have the entire ten commandments stamped onto them. This is quite legal (Coin Code Section 331—title 18—U.S. Government). We buy uncirculated pennies and have them stamped with the commandments. I carry a pocket full of them and say to people I come in contact with, "Here's a little gift for you." You would be amazed at the response. At worst, you will get a "Thank you," and at best people will be overwhelmed. The coin is untouched by human hands and therefore looks as though it's valuable, because of its gold color. I have had people say, "I am going to treasure this."

One lady went into instant prayer (with hands cupped in a prayer position around the coin), and asked if I was a "Father."

If people respond to the coin positively, I then say "This goes with it," and give them a card which says that the first time a coin was stamped in the U.S. was in 1892, and the impression put on the coin was the ten commandments. The card then says the words of the law are illegible, until you turn the coin slightly and let the light reflect on the words. The same applies with the ten commandments. They need the light of the New Testament to show you what the law actually says. Then it goes through the law into grace. Often teenagers show how good their eye-sight is by reading the tiny wording out loud. They do the witnessing for you.

When people try and read the words, it's just a matter of gently asking, "How many have you kept?" Most unsaved people will say, "Most of them." Then you say, "Did you realize that if you lust, the Bible says you've committed adultery in your heart? If you have hatred..." etc.

My friend and pastor, Garry Ansdell and I go into stores, feel the quality of men's shirts and jackets which are on the racks, and quietly drop coins into the pockets—someone's going to find them! I also put them in change slots in public telephones.

During the "relating" process of witnessing, I often build a relationship, and gently break down the person's confidence in his judgments at the same time, with some questions. (These work best verbally, so give this book to someone else and have them ask you these questions; if you just read them yourself, you will fail to see their impact.) Ask any of the following:

1. How many of each animal did Moses take into the ark?
2. What is the name of the raised print that deaf people use?
3. Is it possible to end a sentence with the word "the"?
4. Spell the word "shop." What do you do when you come to a green light?

5. It is noon. You look at the clock. The big hand is on three, the little hand is on five; what time is it?
6. Spell the word "silk." What do cows drink?
7. Listen carefully: You are the driver of a train; there are 30 people on board. At the first stop, 10 people get off. At the next stop, 5 people get on. Now for the question: What is the name of the train driver?

Answers to questions:

1. None. **Moses** didn't take any animals into the ark.
2. Deaf people don't use raised print.
3. The question is an example of one.
4. Go.
5. Noon.
6. Water.
7. **You** are the driver of the train.

Also, experiment with the unsaved using the I.Q. tests straight from this book. If people like them, give the book to them as a gift. They will appreciate it, even if it's just for the tests. If you do give it to them, put their name in it and write "With best wishes," with your own name and the date. You will be delighted at their reaction to the fact that you care enough for them to give them something for nothing.

I trust these thoughts have been helpful to you. Thank you for taking the time to read this book. It is my hope and prayer that you have seen that the ten commandments are truly ten easy ways to see your need of God's forgiveness, and that you will see the necessity to use the law as a schoolmaster to bring sinners to the Savior. May God bless you in your labors for Him and give you the deepest desires of your heart.

Addendum

Here are two sample I. Q. test cards. You may remove them from the book, cut them apart, and reproduce them to use in your evangelistic efforts.

TEST YOUR I.Q.

READ this sentence:

FINISHED FILES ARE THE RE-SULTS OF YEARS OF SCIEN-TIFIC STUDY COMBINED WITH THE EXPERIENCE OF YEARS.

Now count aloud the F's in the box. Count them only ONCE; **do not look back and count them again.** If you think you are right, look on the back.

TEST YOUR I.Q.

Read **OUT LOUD** the wording in the three triangles:

PARIS
IN THE
THE SPRING

BIRD
IN THE
THE HAND

ONCE
IN A
A LIFETIME

Now take a look at the back and see if you are correct:

SIDE TWO. There are six; if you found three, you are average. Here is another intelligence test; answer Yes or No OUT LOUD: **1**/ Is there a God? **2**/ Does God care about right and wrong? **3**/ Are God's standards the same as ours? **4**/ Will God punish sin? **5**/ Is there a Hell? **6**/ Do you avoid Hell by living a good life? The answers are: **1**/Yes. **2**/Yes. **3**/No. **4**/Yes. **5**/Yes. **6**/No. <u>You can't afford to be wrong;</u> find out the truth - ask God to forgive your sins, then trust Jesus Christ, who took your punishment by dying on the cross for you. Read the Bible daily and obey what you read...God will never let you down.
Living Waters Pubns; P.O. Box 1172, Bellflower, CA 90706.

SIDE TWO: The word "the" and "a" are repeated. It's obvious . . . *once you see it.* **Here is another I.Q. Test;** answer Yes or No **OUT LOUD: 1/** Is there a God? **2/** Does God care about right & wrong? **3/** Are God's standards the same as ours? **4/** Will God punish sin? **5/** Is there a Hell? **6/** Do you avoid Hell by living a good life? The answers are, **1/** Yes. **2/** Yes. **3/** No. **4/** Yes. **5/** Yes. **6/** No. *You can't afford to be wrong;* find out the truth - ask God to forgive your sins, then trust Jesus Christ, who took your punishment by dying on the cross for you. Read the Bible daily and obey what you read . . . God will never let you down. **I.Q CARDS, P.O. Box 1172, Bellflower, CA 90706.**